D0226156

Janet Jacobs is Professor of Sociology and Women and Gender Studies, University of Colorado, Boulder. Her publications include *Victimized Daughters: Incest and the Development of the Female Self* (1994), and *Hidden Heritage: The Legacy of the Crypto-Jews* (2002), for which she won the Distinguished Book Award from the Society for the Scientific Study of Religion.

MEMORIALIZING THE HOLOCAUST

GENDER, GENOCIDE AND COLLECTIVE MEMORY

JANET JACOBS

I.B. TAURIS

LONDON · NEW YORK

Published in 2010 by I.B.Tauris & Co. Ltd
6 Salem Road, London W2 4BU
175 Fifth Avenue, New York, NY 10010
www.ibtauris.com

Distributed in the United States and Canada Exclusively by Palgrave
Macmillan
175 Fifth Avenue, NY 10010

Copyright © 2010 Janet Jacobs

The right of Janet Jacobs to be identified as the author of this work has
been asserted by her in accordance with the Copyright, Designs and
Patents Act 1988.

All rights reserved. Except for brief quotations in a review, this book,
or any part thereof, may not be reproduced, stored in or introduced
into a retrieval system, or transmitted, in any form or by any means,
electronic, mechanical, photocopying, recording or otherwise, without
the prior written permission of the publisher.

ISBN: 978 1 84885 102 3 (hardback)
      978 1 84885 103 0 (paperback)

A full CIP record for this book is available from the British Library
A full CIP record for this book is available from the Library of Congress

Library of Congress catalog card: available

Typeset in Perpetua by A. & D. Worthington, Newmarket, Suffolk
Printed and bound in India by Thomson Press India Ltd

CONTENTS

ILLUSTRATIONS

*In memory of the victims of genocide
and human cruelty*

ACKNOWLEDGMENTS

This project took many years to complete. From the early field-work to the final stages of reading and editing, I was supported and encouraged by many close and caring colleagues. The Center for Humanities at the University of Colorado provided my first intellectual explorations into memory studies during my year as a fellow at the Center. I am grateful to all of the other participants in the seminar and especially to Christopher Braider and Jeffrey Cox whose encouragement during this critical phase of the book's development allowed me to see the possibility and importance of the work. I would also like to thank Shawn Landres for easing my entry into Holocaust studies and Emmanuel David for introducing me to the world of visual sociology and with whom I shared many ideas and thoughts as the research evolved. I am grateful to Judy Gerson for reading early drafts of chapters and to Brenda Basher, Joanne Belknap, Donna Goldstein, Karen Jacobs, and Rhys Williams for their careful reading of later versions of the book. The advice and suggestions of my colleagues were invaluable and I greatly appreciate the time and effort they committed to the project.

I am particularly grateful to Patrick Greaney, a Professor in the German and Slavic Language Department at the University of Colorado, who spent many hours with me on German translation and meaning. Additionally, I would like to thank the staff at Ravens-brück Concentration Camp with whom I corresponded and who provided information and texts on the museum exhibits. Their help was invaluable. I am also grateful to Roza Bieliauskiene, Eva Kor, and Sarah Saaroni for sharing their time, wisdom, and vision of memorial culture while I was in the field. I would also like to thank my editor, Philippa Brewster, who stayed with the project and whose dedication to the book made its publication a reality. I am grateful for the editorial assistance of David Worthington, who helped with the final production of this manuscript.

I am especially grateful, as always, to my family—Jamie, Michael, Spencer, and Eric—whose care and encouragement sustained me along the way. Finally, this book would not have been possible without the support, love, and incredible companionship of my life partner, Gary. In embarking on a project such as this, which takes a researcher into painful and tragic landscapes, it is not possible to do it on one's own. From the very beginning, Gary was my travel guide, navigator, and, most importantly, my emotional co-investigator with whom I shared my sorrow, fears, and insights on the many places we studied and the histories we observed. In this sense, the book is truly a collaborative effort, one that could not have been achieved without the love and commitment of a fellow traveler across the time and space of a genocidal past.

INTRODUCTION

THE PROJECT OF MEMORY AND THE STUDY OF THE HOLOCAUST

For over a century, scholars, writers, artists, and thinkers have been interested in and fascinated by the artifacts and meanings of memory. The quest to know and understand how memories are created, how they are coded and retained, and how they shape identity and a sense of self has been at the forefront of Freudian as well as historical and social scientific thought. While the tendency among scholars has been to consider memory as an individual and personal domain, the notion that memory can also have a social, that is, collective component, was first articulated by Émile Durkheim in the *Elementary Forms of Religious Life*. In that classic text, Durkheim describes the way in which group rituals and symbol systems represent the sacred in society and provide the means by which ancestral memory is transmitted across generations. Within this Durkheimian paradigm, ritual culture establishes the context through which collective identity and a shared past is re-inscribed into social consciousness.[1]

Following Durkheim's initial insights on ritualized memory as a distinctly social phenomenon, his student Maurice Halbwachs laid the groundwork for the study of memory as a collective phenomenon and an element of social life. Writing in "The Social Frameworks of Memory,"[2] Halbwachs provides an intellectual justification for the study of memory as a production of social forces, maintaining that:

it is in society that people normally acquire their memories. It is also
in society that they recall, recognize, and localize their memories.
... It is in this sense that there exists a collective memory and social
frameworks for memory; it is to the degree that our individual
thought places itself in these frameworks and participates in this
memory that it is capable of the act of recollection.[3]

Both in "The Social Frameworks of Memory" and a second text,
"The Legendary Topography of the Gospels in the Holy Land,"[4]
Halbwachs elaborates on the role that myths, narratives, and symbol
systems play in the transmission of memory, particularly as social
structures such as the family, religion, and class relations inform the
preservation and dissemination of remembrances of the past. It is
also in these works that Halbwachs identifies the importance of landmarks, social locations, and iconography as sites of memory.

Nearly 60 years after Halbwachs' work first appeared, a plethora of literature on social, cultural, and collective memory began
to emerge in response to the importance of social memory for
contemporary understandings of the present and for the formation
of national and group identity.[5] Within this growing and increasingly complex field, research on the remembrance of mass trauma
has become especially significant, and it is here where the study of
Holocaust memorialization has been at the center of the emerging
scholarship on collective memory. Among the numerous scholars
who are grappling with the meaning of Holocaust memorialization
as an emblem of collective trauma, Jeffrey Alexander suggests that
in memorializing the Holocaust societies seek to create a better and
more just world:

> To create structures that dramatize the tragedy of the Holocaust
> and provide opportunities for contemporaries, now so far removed
> from the original scene, powerfully to re-experience it. ... In each
> Holocaust museum the fate of the Jews functions as a metaphorical
> bridge to the treatment of other ethnic, religious, and racial
> minorities. The aim is manifestly not to "promote" the Holocaust
> as an important event in earlier historical time, but to contribute to
> the possibilities of pluralism and justice in the world today.[6]

Further, as Alexander suggests, with the institutionalization of Holocaust memory in postwar European culture, narratives of good and evil, victim and perpetrator have been widely reproduced in the monuments, museums, and memorials that remember and re-tell the tragedy of Jewish genocide and the violence of Nazi terror.

Over the last two decades, studies of these memorial sites have been numerous and tend to focus especially on Europe, Israel, and the United States, where Holocaust memorials have proliferated and where questions of meaning, politics, and representation have become significant.[7] Among the most important of these studies are the significant works of Sybil Milton and the groundbreaking research by James Young.[8] In 1991 Milton published *In Fitting Memory: The Art and Politics of Holocaust Memorials*, a photographic essay that surveyed Holocaust memorials in Europe, Israel, and the United States. Through imagery and text, the volume presented an evolution of memorial culture, raising critical issues of political context, aesthetics, and cultural difference as each of these dimensions of remembrance informed the development of a collective memory of Nazi genocide. According to Milton, memorialization, especially in Europe, followed three distinct periods that over time led to the expansion and proliferation of a distinctly Holocaust-centered memoryscape in the European imagination.

In the first period, the decade immediately following the war, memorials specifically to Jewish genocide were few in number. Those that were established, such as the gravestone for the Jews at Bergen-Belsen, were either locally initiated or privately sponsored. By the 1960s and 1970s the trend in Holocaust memorialization looked decidedly different. With a greater emotional distance from the Jewish catastrophe, a new political consciousness emerged especially among younger generations in West Germany who sought to recover a suppressed and secreted past. During this time, at the urging of survivor organizations and student groups, markers and commemorative plaques began to appear at deportation sites, destroyed synagogues, cemeteries, and former concentration camps.[9] This period of commemorative activity culminated with the 1979 airing of the US mini-series *Holocaust* in West Germany, during which nearly half the adult population watched one or more episodes.[10] Following the West German broadcast, the final and still evolving era of memorialization began in the 1980s, with greater social awareness of Nazi history and increased media attention—television, film, newspaper, and educational coverage—on the Jewish catastrophe of World War II. This commemorative phenomenon was significantly informed by the fall of the Soviet Union in Eastern Europe and the unification of East and West Germany that followed. Under the Soviet regime, there had been little or no reference to Jewish genocide in the national narratives of World War II. This trend has slowly but significantly changed over the last two decades and, along with the proliferation of museums and memorials more globally, there has been a continued development and revision of Holocaust memorial sites throughout Eastern and Western Europe.[11]

The meaning of these trends in Holocaust memorial culture is the subject of Young's 1993 volume on Holocaust monuments and memorials. In this work, Young looks at what he describes as "the monument's inner life—the tempestuous social, political, and aesthetic forces—normally hidden by a monument's taciturn exterior."[12] To this end, Young's analysis of the memorial phenomenon draws together a visual and cultural narrative of politics, history, place, and Jewish memory that examines the "temporal realm" through which traumatic memory is given form and visibility in the spaces of Holocaust remembrance. Within this powerful and provocative discussion, Young returns to the themes that were first articulated by Halbwachs, reminding the reader that collective memory is after all a social construction whose significance lies not only in the act of remembrance but in the way in which memory functions as a source for shaping national and group identity long after the initial trauma has disappeared from public consciousness.

While the work of Milton and Young provides a foundation from which to build on the study of Holocaust memorialization, this field of research has only recently begun to consider the importance of gender as a category of study within the larger framework of Holocaust memory. Over the last two decades, issues of gender and memory have become particularly salient as feminist scholars have begun to question the way in which women, as a category of remembrance, have been represented in visual and historical narratives of Jewish genocide.[13] As a separate and distinct category of analysis, the study of women in the Holocaust first emerged in the 1980s following a groundbreaking conference on women survivors of Nazi terrorism.[14] Since then there has been a proliferation of gender-based memoirs, testimonies, fictional and non-fictional accounts that, taken together, provide insight into the way in which women's experience of the Holocaust differed from that of men. In addition, the current research on women and the Holocaust includes historical analyses as well as empirical studies that explore, among other phenomena, the role of Jewish women in resistance,[15] the survival strategies of Jewish women in ghettos, Jewish and Christian women in concentration camps,[16] the perpetration of sexual and reproductive crimes against Jewish and Roma (Gypsy) women and girls,[17] and the representation of women in Holocaust narratives and film.[18] The existing research on women under Nazi rule reveals a complex view of the intersection of gender, ethnicity, and genocide. Within the wide range of writings on the Holocaust, women emerge as survivors, victims, resistors, caretakers, and perpetrators—images and archetypes that convey a gendered memory of women within a trauma-based narrative of ethnic violence and mass tragedy.

Although extensive and informative, the existing literature on gender and the Holocaust has yet to illuminate the ways in which these motifs of gendered memory have been incorporated into the monuments and memorials that commemorate Nazi genocide both in Europe and in the transnational Jewish refugee cultures that sought to create their own forms of collective remembrance in the aftermath of World War II. To date the existing work on gender and representation in Holocaust memorials and museums is relatively sparse and focuses primarily on Israel and the US Holocaust Memorial Museum in Washington, DC. In these studies, Judith Tydor Baumel examines motherhood as a symbol of the Holocaust in Israeli national consciousness, while Joan Ringelheim focuses on the issues surrounding the exclusion of women as a separate and distinct victim group in the United States Holocaust Memorial Museum.[19]

More recently, the German scholar and museum curator Insa Eschebach has offered an analysis of Jewish women's representation at the
memorial at the former women's concentration camp at Ravensbrück.[20] These initial studies of women and memory, as well as the
foundational work of Milton and Young, provide a starting point
for my own research in this important area of study. The work that
is presented here explores gender and Holocaust memorialization
within a wide array of cultural settings that illustrate the multifac-
eted nature of Holocaust commemoration and the diverse manifesta-
tions of collective memory.

Research setting and the scope of the project

As an ethnographic study of memorial culture, fieldwork for the
project began in 2001. Using the existing literature on Holocaust
monuments and memorials as well as national, state, and community guides, I identified a wide range of memorialscapes across a vast
expanse of European geographies that included rural and urban areas,
parks and community centers, and the streets of formerly Jewish
neighborhoods. Between 2001 and 2008, I conducted research at
death and labor camps,[21] city and state museums, memorial parks,
places of Jewish life and history, and destroyed synagogues and cemeteries. Following Young, I considered all sites of memory—whether
they be a forest outside of Vilnius or a memorial park in Cologne—
as memorial spaces.

Within this broad definition of memorial culture, the majority of
the research was conducted in Austria, Germany, Poland, and the
Czech Republic, countries where the politics of Holocaust memory
have been especially strong, particularly with the advent of Holocaust tourism and the increased production of memorial structures
and commemorative ceremonies at former sites of Nazi terror. In
addition, I visited two other sites of memory that have been developed and maintained by Holocaust survivors outside Europe. The
inclusion of these memorial spaces, one in the United Sates and
the other in Australia, provide a comparative framework in which

survivor-based memories, rather than national and/or group interests, form the basis for a collective remembrance of Jewish genocide. The definition of collective memory, as it is used in this project, thus encompasses a number of significant dimensions of social remembrance, including what Jeffrey Olick has identified as "aggregated individual recollections," as well as national and state "commemorative activities and production."[22] As a whole, the places of memory that have been included in this study represent a diverse and varied set of monuments and museums where knowledge about the past is conveyed to present generations, where the history of mass trauma is preserved for future understandings of human tragedy, and where the interests and visions of nations, groups, and individuals create multiple narratives for the recollection of Jewish genocide.

Guided by previous studies of collective memory, the initial goals of the research were to examine how memorials and museums to Jewish genocide specifically recalled the memory of women and girls at former sites of terror throughout Eastern and Western Europe. Over time, however, as I became more deeply immersed in the depth and breadth of the memorial landscape, the project expanded to include an analysis of gendered memory that took into account the representations of Jewish men and the tropes of Jewish masculinity that were informed by the memory of the Jewish people as victims and passive participants in their own demise. As the research became more nuanced, examining the feminine as well as masculine tropes of monumentalization, the project became more interdisciplinary in nature. Although I am trained as a sociologist, I turned to the fields of culture and media studies to broaden my understanding of how visual culture and mnemonic symbol systems function in society. In this regard, I am indebted to the work of Marianne Hirsch and Barbie Zelizer, each of whom laid the groundwork for the study of gender, representation, and visual narratives of the Holocaust.[23] At the same time, I also looked to the sociology literature and the increasingly significant subfield of visual sociology. Here I am indebted to the creative initiatives of Howard Becker and a cohort of visual sociologists who have brought a sociological perspective to the study of the visual arts in contemporary society.[24] Weaving together

cultural studies with visual sociological approaches, I have used the
tools of both cultural interpretation and content analysis to explore
and analyze the imagery, visual texts, historical narratives, and artistic renderings that characterize and define the memorial structures
under investigation. In addition, I have also examined published
guides to the memorial sites and museum catalogs for themes of
remembrance and motifs of traumatic memorialization. It is therefore my interpretative framework through which these monuments
and sites have been evaluated and understood.

Further, the work is also informed by my earlier work on trauma
and the role that memory plays in shaping individual as well as collective identity. In my earlier research, I considered the ways in which
the history of the Inquisition became a central theme of identification among modern-day descendants of the Iberian crypto-Jews.[25] In
that study family narratives of persecution were the primary means
by which the historical trauma of forced conversion was transmitted
from one generation to the next. In this project, I have turned to the
public sphere as the place where traumatic memory is coded, stored,
and re-inscribed into individual as well as collective consciousness.
Drawing on the theoretical framework of psychoanalytic thought,
the project is grounded in the supposition that public representations
of trauma and mass violence are internalized by the members of the
society in which these monuments and memorials reside, creating
lasting impressions that then become the basis for the privatization
of traumatic remembrance among those who, in visiting and viewing
these sites, become witnesses to the atrocities of the past.

Thematic content and organizational structure

The book covers six areas of study that range in topic from methods of ethnography to thoughts on the future of memorialization in
a persistently violent world. Throughout the essays in the book, a
feminist perspective has been brought to bear on the analysis of data
and the presentation of the research findings. Within this feminist
framework, questions surrounding the use and misuse of memory are

considered, as well as the unintended consequences that arise from the remembrance of genocidal histories in which women and girls are victimized and through which marginalized men are rendered helpless. As Hirsch and Valerie Smith point out, the relationship between memory studies and feminist studies is longstanding, as each area of research looks to the past to explain the present. As these scholars remind us, bringing a feminist perspective to the study of memory helps to identify the relationships of power that inform the construction of collective memory in both national and community settings.[26]

Starting with a discussion of my own role as a feminist researcher in the field, the study of Holocaust memorialization begins with an interrogation into the feminist ethics of researching the Holocaust at former sites of terror—field settings where the overwhelming evidence of atrocities and extermination challenge the principles of ethnographic subjectivity and the moral value of a gendered reading of ethnic extermination. Chapter 2 then confronts these challenges through a study of representation at Auschwitz. Mindful of the ethical dilemmas that surround the study of genocide, this chapter explores the way in which women's memory is framed by photographs, sculptures, and texts that commemorate starvation, experimentation, captivity, and death. The analysis then turns in Chapter 3 to the women's concentration camp at Ravensbrück and the study of gender in an exclusively women-centered memorial context. In this chapter the definition of the Holocaust is expanded to include all those women—Roma, Sinti, Polish, French, German, Hungarian (as well as other women prisoners of war)—who were tortured, starved, and forced into hard labor and whose lives, like those of the Jewish prisoners, were tragically and traumatically interrupted by the advent of Nazi persecution.

In Chapter 4 the research moves from the concentration and death-camp monuments to sites of terror that mark the spaces of religious violence and the memory of Kristallnacht (The Night of Broken Glass). Here themes of contested masculinity and the emasculation of God are elaborated, as these motifs reveal a complicated and gendered lens through which to recall the 1938 pogroms that destroyed the religious structures of German Jewish life. Following the study of Kristallnacht memorialization, Chapter 5 examines the monuments and museums to pre-nineteenth-century Jewish life that are at the center of Jewish cultural tours in Germany and Eastern Europe. In this analysis, the absence of women as a category of remembrance is interrogated along with the reification of anti-Semitic motifs that both feminize and demonize Jewish men.

Finally, Chapter 6 offers another frame of remembrance in which to consider Holocaust memorialization. Drawing on fieldwork at Holocaust museums in Melbourne, Australia, and Terra Haute, Indiana, this chapter focuses on the creation of memorial spaces by the survivors of Jewish genocide, highlighting the importance of gender to survivor memory and the way in which women's experience informs the construction of visual and textual narratives of mass trauma. The concluding section of this chapter brings together the overall findings of the study with a discussion of collective memory and the ongoing importance of a gendered sensibility for the construction of monuments to atrocities and genocide.

As a study of memorialization, the research that is presented here is, in the end, an exploration into the means by which groups, nations, and individuals bring to public consciousness what is often repressed, hidden, and in many cases denied in the aftermath of war and terror. As such, the memorials that form the basis of this study are, in effect, monuments to a traumatic history in which the private agony of genocide is re-imagined and revealed in collective narratives of horror, loss, shame, guilt, and despair. In bringing the narratives of fear and terror into the spaces of public mourning and awareness, the social structures of Holocaust memory unmask the realities of human brutality and devastation, and thus recall what is possible within the realm of human cruelty. Although the scholarly frame through which this work is presented is that of gender and feminist epistemology, the larger context in which this work is situated is that of the crisis of humanity that the Holocaust represents.

Notes to Introduction

1. Durkheim, Émile, *The Elementary Forms of Religious Life* (Oxford: Oxford University Press, 2001); Misztal, Barbara, "Durkheim on collective memory," *Journal of Classical Sociology* 3 (2003), pp. 125–43; Olick, Jeffrey K., "Collective memory: The two cultures," *Sociological Theory* 17:3 (1999), pp. 333–48.

2. Halbwachs, Maurice, "The Social Frameworks of Memory," in *On Collective Memory* (Chicago: University of Chicago Press, 1992).

3. *Ibid.*, p. 38.

4. Halbwachs, "The Legendary Topography of the Gospels in the Holy Land," in *On Collective Memory* (Chicago: University of Chicago Press, 1992).

5. Connerton, Paul, *How Societies Remember* (London: Cambridge University Press, 1989); Nora, Pierre, *(Lieux de mémoire) Realms of Memory: Rethinking the French Past* (New York: Columbia University Press, 1996); Olick, Jeffrey K. and Daniel Levy, "Collective memory and cultural constraint: Holocaust myth and rationality in German politics," *American Sociological Review* 62 (1997), pp. 921–36; Olick, Jeffrey K. and Joyce Robbins, "Social memory studies: From 'collective memory' to the historical sociology of mnemonic practices," *Annual Review of Sociology* 24 (1998), pp. 105–40; Jeffrey Olick, "Collective memory: The two cultures;" Schwartz, Barry, "The social context of commemoration: A study in collective memory," *Social Forces* 62 (1982), pp. 374–402; Schwartz, Barry, "Social change and collective memory: The democratization of George Washington," *American Sociological Review* 56 (1991), pp. 221–36; Schwartz, Barry, "Memory as a cultural system: Abraham Lincoln in World War II," *American Sociological Review* 61 (1996), pp. 908–27.

6. Alexander, Jeffrey, "On the social construction of moral universes: The Holocaust from war crime to trauma drama," in J. Alexander, R. Eyerman, B. Giesen, N. Smelser, and P. Sztompka (eds), *Cultural Trauma and Collective Memory* (Berkeley: University of California Press, 2004), p. 257.

7. Baumel, Judith Tydor, *Double Jeopardy: Gender and the Holocaust*

(London: Valentine Mitchell, 1998); Carrier, Peter, *Holocaust Monuments and National Memory Cultures in France and Germany since 1989* (New York: Berghahn Books, 2005); Koshar, Rudy, *From Monuments to Traces: Artifacts of German Memory, 1870–1990* (Berkeley: University of California Press, 2000); Lentin, Rona, *Israel and the Daughters of the Shoah: Reoccupying the Territories of Silence* (New York: Berghahn Books, 2000); Leninthal, Edward, *Preserving Memory: The Struggle to Create America's Holocaust Museum* (New York: Viking, 1995); Milton, Sybil, *In Fitting Memory: The Art and Politics of Holocaust Memorials* (Detroit: Wayne State University Press 1991); Stier, Oren and J.S. Landres, (eds), *Religion, Violence, Memory and Place* (Bloomington: University of Indiana Press, 2006); Wiedmer, Caroline, *The Claims of Memory: Representations of the Holocaust in Contemporary Germany and France* (Ithaca: Cornell University Press, 1999); Young, James, *The Texture of Memory: Holocaust Memorials and Meaning* (New Haven: Yale University Press, 1993); Irwin-Zarecka, Iwona, *Frames of Remembrance: The Dynamics of Collective Memory* (New Brunswick, NJ: Transaction Publishers, 1994).

8. Milton, *In Fitting Memory*; Young, *The Texture of Memory*.

9. *Ibid.*

10. This information was obtained from the Museum of Broadcast Communications.

11. Bodemann, Y. Michal (ed), *Jews, Germans, Memory: Reconstructions of Jewish Life in Germany* (Ann Arbor, MI: University of Michigan Press, 1996); Koshar, *From Monuments to Traces*; Milton, *In Fitting Memory*.

12. Young, *The Texture of Memory*, p. 14

13. Baumel, *Double Jeopardy*; Eschebach, Insa, "Engendered oblivion: Commemorating Jewish inmates at the Ravensbrück Memorial," in J.T. Baumel and T. Cohen (eds), *Gender, Place and Memory in the Modern Jewish Experience* (London: Valentine Mitchell, 2003), pp. 126–42; Ofer, Dalia and Lenore Weitzman (eds), *Women in the Holocaust* (New Haven: Yale University Press 1998); Reading, Anna, *The Social Inheritance of the Holocaust: Gender, Culture and Memory* (New York: Palgrave Macmillan, 2002); Ringelheim, Joan, "The split between gender and the Holocaust," in D. Ofer and L. Weitzman (eds), *Women and the Holocaust*, pp. 340–50; Ritter, Carol and John Roth, "Preface," in C. Rittner and J. Roth (eds), *Different Voices: Women and the Holocaust*

(New York: Paragon Press, 1993), pp. xi–xiii; Zelizer, Barbie, "Women in Holocaust photography," in B. Zelizer (ed), *Visual Culture and the Holocaust* (New Jersey: Rutgers University Press, 2001), pp. 247–60.

14. Katz, Esther and Joan Ringelheim, *Proceedings of the Conference: Women Surviving the Holocaust*, Occasional papers from the Institute for Research in History (New York, 1983).

15. Laska, Vera (ed), *Women in the Resistance and in the Holocaust* (Westport: Greenwood Press, 1983); Poznanski, Renee, "Women in the French Jewish underground: Shield bearers of the Resistance?" in D. Ofer and L. Weitzman (eds), *Women in the Holocaust*, pp. 234–52.

16. Baumel, Judith Tydor, "Women's agency and survival strategies during the Holocaust," *Women's International Forum* 22 (1999), pp. 329–47; Bondy, Ruth, "Women in Theresienstadt and the family camp in Birkenau," in D. Ofer and L. Weitzman (eds), *Women and the Holocaust*, pp. 310–26; Karay, Felicja, "Women in the forced labor camps," in D. Ofer and L. Weitzman (eds), *Women in the Holocaust*, pp. 285–309; Unger, Michal, "The status and plight of women in the Lodz ghetto," in D. Ofer and L. Weitzman (eds), *Women in the Holocaust*, pp. 123–42.

17. Gisela, Perl, "A doctor in Auschwitz," in C. Rittner and J. Roth (eds), *Different Voices*, pp. 104–18; Ringelheim, Joan, "Gender and genocide: A split memory," in R. Lentin (ed), *Gender and Catastrophe* (London: Zed Books, 1997), pp. 2–33.

18. Fuchs, Esther (ed), *Women and the Holocaust: Narrative and Representation* (New York: University Press of America, 1999).

19. Baumel, *Double Jeopardy*; Ringelheim, "The split between gender and the Holocaust," in D. Ofer and L. Weitzman (eds), *Women and the Holocaust*.

20. Eschebach, Insa, "Engendered oblivion: Commemorating Jewish inmates at the Ravensbrück Memorial," in J.T. Baumel and T. Cohen (eds), *Gender, Place and Memory in the Modern Jewish Experience*, pp. 126–42.

21. Scholars and historians of the Holocaust distinguish between the death camps of Auschwitz, Majdanek, and Treblinka in Poland that were built primarily for the purpose of extermination, and labor camps, such as Ravensbrück, Buchenwald, Dachau, and Sachsenshausen in Germany,

whose initial purpose was to provide slave labor for the German war effort. In the end, most of the prisoners who were incarcerated in the labor camps, like those who were deported to the death camps, did not survive.

22. Olick, "Collective memory: The two cultures," p. 336.

23. Hirsch, Marianne, *Family Frames: Photography, Narrative and Postmemory* (Cambridge, MA: Harvard University Press, 1997); Zelizer, Barbie, *Visual Culture and the Holocaust* (New Jersey: Rutgers University Press, 2000).

24. Howard, Becker (ed), *Exploring Society Photographically* (Evanston, Ill: Northwestern University Press, 1981); Chapman, Elizabeth, *Sociology and Visual Representations* (New York: Routledge, 1994).

25. See Janet Jacobs, *Hidden Heritage: The Legacy of the Crypto-Jews* (Berkeley: University of California Press, 2002).

26. Hirsch, Marianne and Valerie Smith, "Feminism and cultural memory: An introduction," *Signs: Journal of Women in Culture and Society* 28 (2002), pp. 3–18.

CHAPTER 1

GENOCIDE AND THE ETHICS OF FEMINIST SCHOLARSHIP

More than 20 years ago Judith Stacey wrote a critical essay on feminist methods in which she questioned whether a feminist ethnography was possible.[1] In her provocative discussion, Stacey challenged the widely held view that feminist approaches to ethnographic research mitigated the potentially exploitive aspects of observation and objectification that typified the traditional relationship between the researcher and the population under study. Questioning the assumptions of feminist scholars such as Anne Oakley and Shulamit Reinharz,[2] Stacey suggested that qualitative research methods do not eliminate the dangers associated with hierarchy and scientific "neutrality." Rather, they can pose a somewhat different risk of exploitation, particularly when the researcher is faced with situations such as the death of an informant. Drawing on a fieldwork experience in which such a tragedy occurred, Stacey offered the following critique of feminist ethnography:

> My ethnographic role consigned me to experience this death both as a friend and as a researcher, and it presented me with numerous delicate, confusing dilemmas, such as whether or not and to whom to make a gift of the precious, but potentially hurtful tapes of an oral history I had once constructed with the deceased.

I was confronted as well with the discomforting awareness that as a researcher I stood to benefit from this tragedy. ... This and other fieldwork experiences forced my recognition that conflicts of interest and emotion between the ethnographer as authentic related person (i.e. participant), and as exploiting researcher (i.e. observer) are also an inescapable feature of ethnographic method.[3]

The dilemma that Stacey identified has perhaps even greater relevancy today as feminist research has expanded to include contemporary feminist studies of terrorism, genocide, and collective memory.[4] The self-reflexivity that Stacey brought to bear in her work almost two decades ago therefore offers a starting point from which to consider the current ethical dilemmas that feminist social scientists encounter as they negotiate the difficult moral and emotional terrain of research on gender and the Holocaust.

As a feminist sociologist, I first encountered the ethical challenges of researching cultural memory when I undertook a study of gender representation at Holocaust memorial sites in Eastern Europe. From the outset, this project proved to be especially difficult because I had entered an area of study to which I felt connected both by ethnicity and religion. Over a period of seven years, as I expanded the borders of ethnographic research to include an investigation of numerous and varied Holocaust memorials, I found myself immersed in a research project that not only engendered deep emotional responses but strongly resonated with Stacey's doubts about the possibility of achieving a truly feminist ethnography. In response to the conflicts I experienced as both a participant/Jewish woman and an observer/ social scientist, I engaged in a critical examination of my research methods and goals. This self-reflexive inquiry led to an exploration of the complex ethical issues that inform research on women and genocide specifically and feminist ethnographies of violence more generally. In particular, I identified three sources of tension that were especially pronounced during the research process: role conflicts in the research setting, gender selectivity in studies of ethnic and racial violence, and the sexual objectification of women in academic discourse on violence and genocide. Drawing on my fieldwork in Eastern Europe, my analysis of the data, and my reporting of the findings, this chapter addresses each of these ethical challenges from the standpoint of research on gender and the Holocaust.

The geography of genocide: methods and fieldwork in post-Holocaust Europe

Although there are numerous Holocaust sites located throughout the world, I chose to situate my research primarily in Eastern and Western Europe for two reasons. First, because few studies of European memorial sites had addressed issues of gender, my project was intended to "fill this gap" in Holocaust studies. A second consideration related more specifically to the sites themselves. Unlike Holocaust memorials outside Europe, those within Europe retain what Ulrich Baer refers to as "the experience of place" because they are located in the geographic landscape where the traumatic events actually occurred.[5] Sites such as Auschwitz thus bring a realism and authenticity to the memorial space. It was this realism that I sought to understand and examine as I explored the social construction of women's memory.

My fieldwork in Europe began at Theresienstadt in the Czech Republic. A former concentration camp that was touted as a "model" prison by the Germans, Theresienstadt is a nineteenth-century fortress which, located on the outskirts of Prague, was used as a prisoner of war camp during World War II. The camp has since been preserved as a memorial site to Czech resistance fighters as well as other groups, including Jews, who were deemed unfit or a threat to German occupation. Maintained essentially as a war memorial, the structures at Theresienstadt have not been changed or refurbished in any way. The markings and suffering of the former prisoners are still visible in the wooden bunks and broken furniture that define the memorial space. Each section of the camp—the kitchen, the latrines, and the torture rooms—contain narratives in Czech, German, and English that, with great detail, describe the German occupation of the former Czechoslovakia and the crimes that were committed against the Czechs. As such, Theresienstadt is a powerful first encounter with the remembrance of Nazi atrocities, reminding visitors that the Jews, while the primary target of genocide, were part of a larger effort at German domination and political repression.

A few miles from this prison camp, however, the memorial to Terezin, the Jewish ghetto, tells quite a different story. The brick buildings of Terezin, now a Holocaust museum, comprise the remaining areas of the ghetto to which Jews were sent prior to their deportation to Auschwitz. Unlike the nearby prisoner of war camp, the dominant memory at Terezin is that of Jewish incarceration and suffering. Among the most prominent installations are those that focus especially on the experience of women and children. It was here that Friedl Dicker-Brandeis organized art classes for the children of the ghetto whose fears and anxieties became the subject for drawings and paintings that now hang on the walls of the buildings and have been reprinted in a poignant text, *i have not seen a butterfly here.*[6] It is also here where women, faced with increasing food shortages, created meals out of ghetto rations, the recipes for which have been published in *In Memory's Kitchen*, a cookbook of Holocaust remembrance that provides another artifact of Jewish women's lives under Nazi rule.[7] Because women and children's experiences were at the center of Holocaust representations at Terezin, this site offered my first glimpse into the gendered nature of memorial culture, a theme that I would return to over the next seven years as I expanded my research from the Czech Republic to Poland and eventually to the numerous and diverse memorials of Central and Western Europe.

Throughout my fieldwork, I approached these varied and diverse memorial spaces from the subject position of both a participant (Jewish woman) and an empathic observer (feminist ethnographer). In my role as participant, I recited the Jewish prayer of mourning, placing stones on the graves and crematoria where Jews and other victims of the Holocaust had died. As feminist ethnographer, I observed and recorded the remnants, especially of women's lives, that were recalled and remembered in the museums and memorial structures. Thus at the same time that I deeply felt the pain of a more universal Jewish trauma, I specifically looked for evidence of women's Holocaust experience. To this end, I searched for women's names on memorial plaques that had been placed at massacre sites, I looked for women's clothing and artifacts in museum displays and dioramas, and I sought out images of women in photographs and in the government narratives that provided information on the history and victims of internment.

As the research progressed and the experience especially at the death camps grew more intense and emotional, my dual roles as participant and observer became more problematic. Increasingly, I became uncomfortably aware of the moral implications of interrogating gender and genocide for the purposes of research and scholarly productivity. Because my research resides at the intersection of Jewish memory and ethnic extermination, my multiple identities were at times in contention with one another as the ethical responsibility attached to each role had distinct and different parameters. While I felt a moral responsibility to encode the victim's suffering into my own ethnic memory, my stance as observer demanded a certain distancing from the horrors of the past. In negotiating the tenuous moral terrain between empathic identification with the victims and the viewing of their dehumanization and death for the purposes of research, I grappled with the meaning of bearing witness, as this form of moral observation is deeply rooted in Holocaust remembrance. During this stage of the research project, my field notes spoke of my confusion over bearing witness to Jewish genocide while engaging in a process of data gathering through which I was creating a personal archive of genocidal history.

Role conflicts: the researcher as witness and the problem of double vision

In what may be the most provocative interpretation of post-Holocaust witnessing to date, Marianne Hirsch suggests that those who currently view images of Nazi atrocities become witnesses to the crimes.[8] Drawing specifically on late twentieth-century Holocaust exhibits, Hirsch calls into question the moral culpability of the observer who becomes witness to these atrocities centuries later. In particular, Hirsch cites a photographic exhibit in which four women are shown in their underclothes as they are about to be executed. Hirsch suggests that while the camera is in a similar position to that of the gun, the photographer is in the same place as the unseen executioner. Because the women in this exhibit are "doubly exposed in their nakedness and powerlessness,"[9] Hirsch asks:

> How are postmemorial viewers to look at this picture and others like it? Where are the lines of transgenerational identification and empathy? Unbearably the viewer is positioned in the place identical with the weapon of destruction: our look, like the photographer's, is in the place of the executioner. ... Is it possible to escape the touch of death and the implication of murder that these images perform?[10]

The ethical questions that Hirsch raises have particular relevance for the feminist ethnographer who engages in the viewing and recording of images of death and violence. As a "secondary" witness to atrocities, the ethnographer enters into an ambiguous moral relationship to her subjects. I have characterized this dilemma as the problem of "double vision," wherein the researcher is at once both a witness to crimes against humanity and an ethnographic observer in search of qualitative data. As a witness to crimes against humanity, the researcher enters into a deeply personal relationship with her subjects that, according to Dori Laub, often obscures the boundaries between the researcher and the researched, a blurring of subjectivity that is intensified by bonds of gender and ethnic kinship. Historical scholars of the Holocaust have approached this troubling aspect of Holocaust studies from the standpoint of psychoanalytic thought. Dominick LaCapra, for example, suggests that "The Holocaust presents the historian with transference in the most traumatic form conceivable," wherein the persecution and suffering of the subjects give rise to unconscious feelings and reactions in the scholar.[11] Saul Friedlander describes the transferential phenomenon as follows:

the major difficulties of historians of the *Shoah*, when confronted with echoes of the traumatic past, is to keep some measure of balance between the emotion recurrently breaking through the "protective shield" and numbness that protects this very shield. In fact, the numbing or distancing effect of intellectual work on the *Shoah* is unavoidable and necessary; the recurrence of strong emotional impact is also often unforeseeable and necessary.[12]

The ethnographer who studies Holocaust memory is similarly immersed in the historical realism of Nazi atrocities and is thus vulnerable to the emotional strains of witnessing catastrophe within the context of scholarly research. As a Jewish woman studying the extermination of other Jewish women, I therefore found myself vacillating between the extremes of an almost paralyzing empathy and the distancing that my engagement in the research process would allow. Although I never quite experienced the numbing that Friedlander describes, my defense against the horror took form in my use of the camera as a research tool.

In entering the field of memorial culture, I chose photography as a means of data gathering at the Holocaust sites. Photography facilitated the construction of a "portable" database that could be transferred from the emotion-laden research setting (the Holocaust site) to the comparatively safe haven of my office in the United States. I videotaped the interior of concentration camp buildings and I took photographs of the walls and displays, recording images and artifacts of women that I could later analyze when I returned home. It was during this phase of the research project—the creation of a photographic archive—that the tensions of "double vision" began to materialize. In positioning the camera to record the images under investigation, my initial responses of empathy and moral outrage gave way to more pragmatic concerns over lighting, color, and contrast. At these moments in the research process, the subjects became objects to be viewed through the camera's lens, their humanity and victimization secondary to the needs of observation and data gathering.

These potentially dehumanizing aspects of the ethnographic project were particularly pronounced at Auschwitz where the museum photographs are, in many cases, those that originally had been taken by the Nazis to document medical experiments and other forms of torture and deprivation. In retaking these photographs decades later for the purposes of research on collective memory, I questioned whether I had unwittingly replicated the acts of the perpetrators who had also photographed these women in order to create an archive of genocidal history. In witnessing the atrocities through the lens of the social scientist's camera, had I, as Hirsch suggests, become implicated in the original crime, subordinating the memory and pain of the victim to the goals of scientific inquiry? Although I reassured myself that, unlike the Nazi perpetrators, my research objectives would restore integrity and respect to the memory of the photographed subjects, I remain haunted by the possibility that I am nevertheless "tainted" by my role as observer and my use of photography as a data-gathering tool.

In retrospect, I recognize that my ability to create an intellectual space in the midst of traumatizing imagery and artifacts was, to a large extent, dependent on the shifts in perspective that my use of photography demanded. The camera thus became a vehicle for my separation from the subjects, a distancing that, while facilitating the management of emotions in the field, also challenged the values of empathy and closeness in which much of feminist ethnography is grounded.[13] Although feminist methodological approaches have for the most part tended to emphasize closeness rather than distance in the field, a number of feminist scholars have begun to address the difficulties that closeness with the subjects may impose on the research process.[14] The sociologist Lynn Davidman, for example, thoughtfully discusses a struggle to separate her life experiences and assumptions from those of her subjects during a study of newly Orthodox women:

> Since a central goal of this project was to convey, as best as I could, the women's attraction to Orthodox Judaism from the perspective of their life experiences and social locations and not from mine,

I knew I needed some help in sorting out my personal reactions. Otherwise, these feelings would prevent me from seeing and hearing realities that differed from my own, and my research project would be a failure. I worked for over a year with a therapist to separate out my memories and feelings of being forced by my father to attend services and observe Jewish law and practices, from the realities of the women who made a conscious choice to be in the synagogue every Shabbat morning.[15]

For Davidman, the success of the project relied on her ability to separate her intrusive memories and emotions from the research perspectives that she brought to the fieldwork setting. In my own research, the issues surrounding closeness and separation from the subjects emerged in a somewhat different context. I feared that in creating and sustaining emotional distance from the women, I would be at risk for exploiting their pain and degradation. As these fears emerged and re-emerged at each site that I visited, I used my field notes both as a therapeutic aid and a confessional where I acknowledged my doubts about the ethics of the study. The self-reflection and introspection that the field notes allowed provided a method with which I constantly assessed the goals and objectives of the work against the exploitation of an atrocity history to which I felt so closely allied. As I painstakingly recorded the personal conflicts that accompanied my shifts in vision between subjective witnessing and objectifying data collection, other moral issues also began to surface, most notably those having to do with the ethics of victim selectivity in Holocaust research.

Engendering the Holocaust: the moral complexities of victim selectivity in studies of genocide

Holocaust scholars disagree over whether women and men should be considered as two distinct populations in the study of ethnic destruction. Writers such as Ruth Bondy and Lawrence Langer, for example, challenge the notion that women should be studied separately in historical and social analyses of mass extermination.[16] Although Bondy offers insight into women's experience at Theresienstadt in a volume specifically on women and the Holocaust, she qualifies her discussion with the following introductory remarks:

> Zykon B [lethal gas] did not differentiate between men and women; the same death swept them all away. Because the same fate awaited all Jews, I approached the writing of this chapter with grave reservations: why should I focus on women? Any division of the Holocaust and its sufferers according to gender seemed offensive to me. This issue of gender seemed to belong to another generation, another era.[17]

Similarly, in his study of women and suffering, Langer challenges the moral stance of what he perceives as the privileging of one group over another in Holocaust studies:

> The pain of loss and the relief of survival remain entwined in the memory of those lucky enough to have outlived the atrocities. All efforts to find a rule of hierarchy in that darkness, whether based on gender or will, spirit or hope, reflect only our own need to plant a life sustaining seed in the barren soil that conceals the remnants of two-thirds of European Jewry. The sooner we abandon this design, the quicker we will learn to face such chaos with unshielded eyes.[18]

In contrast to these points of view, feminist scholars such as Lenore Weitzman, Dalia Ofer, Carol Rittner, and Joan Ringelheim maintain that the study of women in the Holocaust is not only valid but necessary to redress the absence of women's lives and experiences in the documentation of Holocaust history and the preservation of Holocaust memory.[19] Rittner and Roth state that:

> relatively little attention has been paid to women's experiences before, during or after the Holocaust. Much of the best witness literature by women, the autobiographical accounts of those who survived the Holocaust is out of print or not easily accessible. Much

of the most widely read scholarship—historical, sociopolitical, philosophical, and religious—treats the Holocaust as if sexual and gender differences did not make a difference. ... Thus the particularities of women's experiences and reflections have been submerged and ignored.[20]

Further, Ringelheim argues for the inclusion of women-centered perspectives that focus on "gender-specific" traumas such as sexual assault and reproductive abuse. As such, she asserts that, "For Jewish women the Holocaust produced a set of experiences, responses, and memories that do not always parallel those of Jewish men."[21]

Having been involved in feminist research for close to 20 years, I welcomed this gendered approach to the study of genocide, and was thus inspired to engage in my own studies of women and the Holocaust. For this research project in particular, I brought what I construed to be "a feminist gaze" to the study of women's representation, a visual lens through which the memory of women's lives, experiences, and suffering could be explored within the context of public memorials and museums. Although I was somewhat interested in the question of inclusion, that is, the extent to which women were represented in these memorial venues, I was especially drawn to visual content, the way in which women's stories of genocide were told through the imagery and artifacts that have become part of the public memory of Holocaust trauma.

As I became increasingly engaged in the ethnography, however, I became more troubled by the moral tensions that the fieldwork raised. I began to have a greater appreciation for those who objected to a gendered analysis of the Holocaust, particularly in Eastern Europe where sites such as Auschwitz and Majdanek offer an almost incomprehensible memory of ethnic subjugation and cultural annihilation. These "living" gravesites contain the artifacts, photographs, and human remains of millions of women, children, and men whose memory provides the focal point for the exhibition halls and memorial spaces. Approaching these sites from the perspective of women's representation requires the observer to focus her attention primarily on woman-centered imagery and atrocities, a subjective point of view in which the women become larger, more obvious in their degradation, suffering and humiliation, while the men recede into the ethnographic background. My observation and analysis of the visual representations of the tattooed female body is illustrative of this troubling phenomenon.

In a collage-like exhibit at Auschwitz, tattooed limbs of the prisoners are preserved in photographic imagery in which only an arm or leg are visible, highlighting the numbers imprinted on the exposed body part. Among these images, only one limb belonging to a woman is discernible. In this photograph, the female prisoner's knee is slightly bent, her body in profile, revealing the numbers that had been burned into her upper thigh. The upper limits of the photograph are bounded by a skirt which appears to have been raised intentionally for the camera. Had this image stood alone, separate from the other more masculine arms and legs, it might be mistaken for a 1940s pornographic postcard.

As a visual memory of Auschwitz, however, this image of ethnic branding conveys a kind of sadomasochistic eroticism that is absent from the tattooed depictions of the male prisoners.[22] It is thus the singular image of the woman's thigh that I chose for my photographic archive, an image that in its gendered representation offers evidence of the objectification of the Jewish female body in Holocaust memory. In reviewing this and other photographs of Auschwitz, I could not ignore the obvious reality that in the pursuit of feminist research goals I had relegated Jewish men to a place of insignificance. For the purposes of my research, the memory of the men as victims of death and ethnic branding was important only in so far as their bodies offered a background against which to compare the women. Through a process of ethnographic selectivity, I therefore chose which memory to privilege and which to trivialize, a choice that, in the face of genocidal histories, raises serious ethical concerns.

Similarly, in the rooms that house the installations of artifacts and Jewish memorabilia—hair, clothing, and religious objects—I became increasingly aware of the absence of the memory of women as religious Jews. In comparison with the men, there is little evidence of their religious lives in the remnants that had been carefully preserved and displayed at the camps. With the exception of Sabbath candlesticks, most of the religious artifacts in the museums relate specifically to male culture—prayer shawls, skull caps, and phylacteries—that signify the religious observance of Jewish men in prewar Eastern European. These observations led me to conclude that while the remembrance of religious genocide is presented primarily through the frame of male ritual and practice, the memory of ethnic genocide is most often recalled through images of the subjugated female body, photographs of naked and starved women whose memory has come to represent the worst of Nazi atrocities. Thus in observing and recording the remnants of victims' belongings at memorial sites such as the death camp at Majdanek, my attention was especially drawn to the thousands of women's shoes that have been preserved in massive iron cages which, since the 1940s, have been used to house the clothing and confiscated possessions of the murdered victims.

While Auschwitz is perhaps the best-known and most frequently visited concentration camp museum and memorial, Majdanek is the more historically authentic of the two World War II sites. Situated in the southeastern part of the country, Majdanek is surrounded by high-rise apartment buildings that overlook the grounds and buildings of the former death camp. The approach to Majdanek is marked by a huge stone sculpture that, according to James Young, is intended to convey a sense of danger that infuses past events as well as present memories.[23] Once inside the camp, however, it is the memory of genocide that becomes pervasive and overwhelming. Opposite the entrance to the camp ground, at the end of a long road, a dome-shaped mausoleum houses the ashes of the 350,000 mostly Jewish victims who died at Majdanek. This powerful gravesite provides a backdrop to the rows of wooden barracks, abandoned guard houses, and barbed-wire fences that today comprise the infrastructure of the museum. In entering Majdanek, perhaps more so than in any other Holocaust site, the visitor is returned to an almost unaltered landscape of horror and death, a geography of remembrance that seems untouched by the passage of history and the intervention of time.

Especially in entering the shoe exhibit, the observer is transported to another time and place where the reality of genocide immediately assaults the senses, as smells of dust and aging leather converge to create a memory of ethnic crimes.[24] Searching among the victims' relics at Majdanek, I immediately looked for women's artifacts, recording the way in which the women's shoes stood out, the expensive evening wear and the worn-out sandals making a stark contrast to the less colorful and less evocative men's foot coverings (Figure 1). As I carefully and painstakingly documented the remnants of the women's shoes, I once again became engaged in a process of selection. Through the lens of my camera, the men's work shoes became the backdrop against which the silk high heels and peasant women's boots were framed. Even the numerous and tragic children's shoes were relegated to a place of secondary importance in the photographic compositions that I recorded for analysis. Both at the Holocaust site and then later at home, with the photographs strewn across my desk, I experienced a "crisis" of observation in which I not only questioned my betrayal of Jewish men and children but my responsibility for a research project that, by its very nature, could contribute to the dissemination of images of women's subjugation and degradation that were already so pervasive in Holocaust memorial culture.

Modes of representation: academic voyeurism and the reporting of data

The photographs I took of the shoe installation at Majdanek, along with those of the tattooed and starved bodies at Auschwitz, contributed to a database of atrocity images with which I began the arduous and painful process of data analysis. As I cataloged the hundreds of images that I had collected during my years of fieldwork—coding each photograph according to content, place, and historical context—patterns of representation began to emerge. From the outset, I observed that women appeared to be over-represented in atrocity images and artifacts at sites such as Auschwitz and Majdanek. Although men are strongly represented in the museum exhibitions and installations, it is primarily women's bodies that

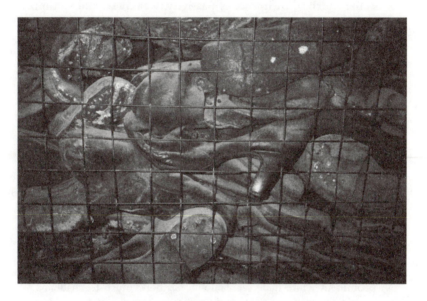

1. Shoe installation at Majdanek.

form the focal point for the commemoration of atrocities, such as human experimentation, that highlight the violation and desecration of the Jewish body. Having arrived at this disturbing conclusion, I was then faced with the dilemma of how best to report and present these results without using graphic illustrations that, while convincing, would reify and re-inscribe these images into public consciousness. Because recent as well as past research on Holocaust representation has contributed to the persistence of a Jewish memory that is characterized by images of passivity, weakness, and victimization, I was especially wary of reinforcing this form of remembrance, as such studies invite a kind of observational voyeurism, especially when gender is the focus of the analysis.

Patricia Hill Collins and Anne Fausto-Sterling discuss this problem of scientific reporting in each of their works on Black women and the racialized body.[25] In particular, Hill Collins discusses the dangers of using female imagery in academic presentations that are geared toward exposing scientific racism. Speaking specifically of studies of Sarah Bartmann, the so-called Hottentot Venus who was exhibited in Paris during the nineteenth century, Hill Collins cites the academic setting as the place in contemporary culture where Bartmann has once again become the object of a racialized and gendered gaze:

> A prominent white male scholar who has done much to challenge scientific racism apparently felt few qualms at using a slide of Sarah Bartmann as part of his Powerpoint presentation. Leaving her image on screen for several minutes with a panel of speakers that included Black women seated on stage in front of the slide, this scholar told jokes about the seeming sexual interests of White voyeurs of the nineteenth century.[26]

Hill Collins further describes another presentation in which Bartmann's image was used by Black male scholars to illustrate the changing physiology of the Black body. As in the example cited above, Bartmann became the focus for a slide show that, according to Collins, "allowed a lengthy voyeuristic peek" at the "raced" body.[27]

In drawing attention especially to the victimized bodies of Jewish women, studies of gender representation of the Holocaust risk promoting a similar form of academic voyeurism that, however unintentional, contributes to a literature on genocide in which the violated Jewish female is re-inscribed in post-Holocaust memory. In surveying studies on gender representation of the Holocaust, the important work of Barbie Zelizer provides a lens through which to interrogate this dilemma of academic reporting.[28] In her compelling and groundbreaking analysis of woman and Holocaust imagery, Zelizer analyzed the news media's depiction of women immediately following the liberation of the concentration camps. Her survey of atrocity photographs indicates that women were pictured as survivors, perpetrators, witnesses, and victims. Further, Zelizer found that images of women were used to convey the depth of the atrocities and to universalize genocide:

> Perhaps because women were presumed to be more vulnerable than men, the brutality both against women and by women was seen as doubly atrocious, challenging gender-based expectations of humanity. Not surprising then, female gender was strategically emphasized in the photographic record of the camps that emerged.[29]

While Zelizer concludes that women's victimization became the symbolic representation of Nazi brutality and destruction, her analysis also shows that certain images of women, those that had an especially erotic component, were frequently excluded from the mass dissemination of photographs of women. In particular, she discusses a photograph that shows the corpse of a nude woman whose body was found near her two dead children when the allied troops entered the death camp at Bergen-Belsen. Zelizer points out that while the imagery of the two dead children was widely circulated, the partially clothed body of their mother was routinely cropped from the newspaper pictures, leading Zelizer to conclude that the mother's image, both beautiful and sexual, violated the more domesticated representations of victimization that were favored by the press:

In these images, bodies of women were strewn alongside those of children, in scenes depicting a kind of warped domesticity. One such image was taken at Belsen, and it appeared in the *Saturday Evening Post* and the British journal *Picture Post*. Readers were told that it portrayed a brother and sister who had starved to death. But a corresponding shot, which extended from the children's bodies, revealed that of their naked mother lying on the ground nearby. ... Why was one photo widely reproduced and the other accompanying it was not? It may have been that the woman of the latter shot—the mother of the dead children—was considered too beautiful and perhaps erotic to be shown.[30]

To illustrate her point, Zelizer includes the photograph of the dead woman in her textual analysis. While her argument is strengthened by the inclusion of this provocative image, the dissemination of the graphic illustration nonetheless raises a number of ethical concerns. Because Zelizer presents this section of the photograph alone, decontextualized from the corresponding images of her dead children or the topology of the death camp in which her body lies, its inclusion in the essay unintentionally offers an eroticized vision of the Jewish female victim that makes possible the kind of academic voyeurism to which Hill Collins refers.

Given the imagery of sexualized victimization that comprises my own gendered archive of Holocaust remembrance, I am torn between presenting the photographic evidence and withholding these images from public view. While Zelizer appropriately questions the suppression of one particular image of the maternal body in postwar Holocaust photographs, I would expand the discussion to include an analysis of how the use of such images raises other issues, most notably the sexual exploitation of women's suffering in public remembrance of ethnic trauma and catastrophe. Particularly after doing the fieldwork in Eastern Europe, I have become increasingly concerned about the voyeuristic consequences of bringing these images into the public arena of academic discourse. Because I am speaking for and representing the dead, women to whom I feel connected both by gender and ethnicity, I am especially cognizant of the ways in which my research shapes the memory of the subjects, women who have been remembered and memorialized essentially as embodied victims of ethnic genocide, nameless, without humanity, religiosity, or individuality. I am acutely aware of my responsibility to sustain a dignified memory of the Jewish women who died at the camps, particularly because I am interrogating the ways in which the subjugation of their bodies has become a form of public record and the vehicle through which the history of Nazi atrocities is remembered and represented at Holocaust sites throughout Eastern Europe. Thus, here and elsewhere in the reporting of my research, I, like Hill Collins and Fausto-Sterling, have chosen narrative and description, rather than the photographic images of the victims, to convey the brutalized memory of their suffering. Where I have included illustrations, these images are primarily of sculptures and other visual texts that, while figurative pieces, are one step removed from the realism of victim-based atrocity pictures.

Finally, since the inception of the research project, I have time and again returned to Stacey's question, asking myself whether a feminist ethnography of Holocaust representation is actually possible. In answer to her own quandary, Stacey suggested that, while the methods of ethnography preclude the possibility of a totally feminist research process, a "partial" feminist ethnography, in which the moral consequences of representing the Other is addressed, is both a worthwhile and necessary scholarly endeavor.[31] In the case of Holocaust memorial culture, I cautiously agree with Stacey's conclusions. The atrocities of the Holocaust must somehow be remembered and conveyed into post-Holocaust memory. It is thus the responsibility of the feminist scholar to interrogate not only the gendered realities of ethnic annihilation but the problems inherent in representing the victimization of women through the lens of socio-cultural objectification.

Through an interrogation into my own research process, I have sought to examine the varied and significant ethical issues that have yet to be resolved in such feminist endeavors. Throughout the research process, I made a number of choices that allowed me to complete the fieldwork, even as I wrestled with the dilemmas and issues that I have described here. Most significantly, I chose to complete the research project as originally conceived, maintaining my focus on women and using photography as a data-gathering tool. In addition, because of the relationship between women's and men's memory, I also decided, in the initial phases of the study, to expand the scope of the project to include an examination of the issues surrounding representations of Jewish masculinity and thus, through representational discourse, address the victimization of Jewish men in Holocaust remembrance. I made these decisions in the field primarily because of the startling content of the imagery. Weighing the potential importance of the findings against the ethical consideration of the data-gathering process, I became reconciled to the moral discomfort of "double vision." At the same time, my emotional experiences and moral difficulties with the Holocaust study have led me to re-evaluate how to discuss and present my data without further exploiting Jewish tragedy and the memory of Jewish suffering. In the chapters that follow, I hope to remain true to my own intellectual honesty while preserving, with sensitivity and respect, the memory of those whose violation and threatened religious culture have been so extensively memorialized in the collective imagination of a post-Holocaust world.

Notes to Chapter 1

1. Stacey, Judith, "Can there be a feminist ethnography?" *Women's Studies International Forum* 11 (1988), pp. 21–7.

2. Oakley, Anne, "Interviewing women: A contradiction in terms," in H. Roberts (ed), *Doing Feminist Research* (London: Routledge, 1981); Reinharz, Shulamit (with Lynn Davidman), *Feminist Methods in Social Research* (New York: Oxford University Press, 1992).

3. Stacey, Judith., "Can there be a feminist ethnography?," p. 23.

4. Boose, Lynda. "Crossing the River Drina: Bosnian rape camps, Turkish impalement, and Serb cultural memory," *Signs: A Journal of Women, Culture and Society* 28 (2002), pp. 20–38; Lentin, Ronit (ed), *Gender and Catastrophe*.

5. Baer, Ulrich, "To give memory a place: Holocaust photography and landscape tradition," *Representations* 69 (2000), p. 42.

6. Frankova, Anita, *i have not seen a butterfly here* (Prague: The Jewish Museum, 1993).

7. DeSilva, Cara, *In Memory's Kitchen: A Legacy from the Women of Terezin* (New Jersey: Jason Aronson, 1996).

8. Hirsch, Marianne, "Surviving images: Holocaust photographs and the work of postmemory," in B. Zelizer (ed), *Visual Culture and the Holocaust*, pp. 215–42.

9. *Ibid.*, p. 233.

10. *Ibid.*

11. LaCapra, Dominick, "Representing the Holocaust: Reflections on the historian's debate," in S. Friedlander (ed), *Probing the Limits of Representation: National Socialism and the "Final Solution"* (Cambridge: Harvard University Press, 1992), p. 110.

12. Friedlander, Saul, *Memory, History and the Extermination of the Jews in Europe* (Bloomington: University of Indiana Press, 1996).

13. DeVault, Marjorie, *Liberating Method: Feminism and Social Research* (Philadelphia: Temple University Press, 1998); Reinharz, *Feminist Methods in Social Research*.

14. Behar, Ruth, "Writing in my father's name: A diary of *Translated Woman's* first year," in R. Behar and D.A. Gordon (eds), *Women Writing*

Culture (Berkeley: University of California Press, 1995), pp. 65–101; Davidman, Lynn, "Truth, subjectivity and ethnographic research," in J. Spikard and S. Landres (eds), *Personal Knowledge and Beyond* (New York University Press, 2002), pp. 17–26; Wolf, Diane, *Beyond Anne Frank: Hidden Children and Postwar Families in Holland* (Berkeley: University of California Press, 2007).

15. Davidman, Lynn, "Truth, subjectivity and ethnographic research," in J. Spikard and S. Landres (eds), *Personal Knowledge and Beyond*, pp. 24–5.

16. Bondy, Ruth, "Women in Theresienstadt and the family camp in Birkenau," in D. Ofer and L. Weitzman (eds), *Women and the Holocaust* (New Haven: Yale University Press 1998), pp. 310–26; Langer, Lawrence, "Gendered suffering? Women in Holocaust testimonies," in D. Ofer and L. Weitzman (eds), *Women and the Holocaust*, pp. 351–63.

17. Bondy, Ruth, "Women in Theresienstadt and the family camp in Birkenau," p. 310.

18. Langer, Lawrence, "Gendered suffering? Women in Holocaust testimonies," p. 362.

19. Ofer and Weitzman (eds), *Women and the Holocaust*; Ringelheim, Joan, "The split between gender and the Holocaust," in *Women and the Holocaust*, pp. 340–50; Rittner, Carol and John Roth (eds), *Women and the Holocaust: Different Voices* (New York: Paragon, 1993).

20. Rittner and Roth, *Women and the Holocaust: Different Voices*, p. xi.

21. Ringelheim, "The split between gender and the Holocaust," in Ofer and L. Weitzman (eds), *Women and the Holocaust*, p. 350.

22. It is of interest to note that a similar exhibit at the Holocaust Memorial Museum in Washington, DC, contains photographs of men's arms only, multiple images of tattooed forearms and musculature displayed in a collage-like mural that comprises a large portion of one wall. Here the gender selectivity is in the eyes of the curator rather than the ethnographer.

23. Young, James, *The Texture of Memory: Holocaust Memorials and Meanings* (New Haven: Yale University Press, 1993).

24. The shoe exhibit at Majdanek was the inspiration for the shoe installation at the Holocaust Memorial Museum in Washington, DC. The shoe relics in the US museum were transported from Majdanek to

Washington, DC, for the permanent exhibit.

25. Hill Collins Patricia, *Black Feminist Thought: Knowledge, Consciousness, and Empowerment* (Boston: Unwin Hyman, 1990); Fausto-Sterling, Anne, "Gender, race, and nation: The contemporary anatomy of 'Hottentot' Women in Europe, 1815–1817," in J. Terry and J. Urla (eds), *Deviant Bodies* (Bloomington: Indiana University Press, 1995), pp. 19–48.

26. Hill Collins, *Black Feminist Thought: Knowledge, Consciousness, and Empowerment*, p. 142.

27. *Ibid.*

28. Zelizer, Barbie, "Women in Holocaust photography," in B. Zelizer (ed), *Visual Culture and the Holocaust* (New Jersey: Rutgers University Press, 2001), pp. 247–60.

29. *Ibid.*, p. 255

30. *Ibid.*, pp. 257–8.

31. Stacey, "Can there be a feminist ethnography?".

CHAPTER 2

GENDER AND COLLECTIVE MEMORY: WOMEN AND REPRESENTATION AT AUSCHWITZ

As a site of memorial culture, Auschwitz holds a distinct place in the memory of the Holocaust. As the most well-known and frequently visited death-camp memorial, it is a place of remembrance where over half of the victims were Jewish women and children.[1] Within a year of the camp's liberation, the creation of a museum/memorial at the site was begun by former Polish prisoners who returned to the abandoned camp grounds with the goal of establishing a memorial to those who had suffered and died there.[2] Among the artifacts and ruins that were found at the camp were pictures that had been taken by the camp photographers who, themselves prisoners of war, helped to develop a photographic archive that documented the identities of the prisoners and the horrific experiments that were conducted by Josef Mengele. It was these photographs that were used in the trials at Nuremberg and that were placed on display as the first exhibitions in the postwar memorial space.[3] Over the next two decades, under the auspices of the national parliament, Auschwitz became a significant site of memory for the Polish nation. In keeping with Soviet-era ideologies of national remembrance, the museum/memorial space highlighted the camp's history with regard to political prisoners, Polish resistance fighters, and the sacrifice and bravery of the Soviet liberators.[4] Little of these textual narratives referred to ethnic genocide. This oversight persisted until the dismantling of the Soviet Union when new textual material, created in collaboration with Jewish groups, was carved into stone tablets that today mark the entry to the camp. The new text reframes the history of Auschwitz as a site of mass extermination:

> Throughout the world, Auschwitz has become a symbol of terror, genocide, and the Holocaust. ... The first people to be brought to Auschwitz as prisoners and murdered here were Poles. They were followed by Soviet prisoners of war, Gypsies and deportees of many other nationalities. Beginning in 1942, however, Auschwitz became the setting for the most massive murder campaign in history, when the Nazis put into operation their plan to destroy the entire Jewish population of Europe. The great majority of Jews who were deported to Auschwitz – men, women and children – were sent upon arrival to death in the gas chambers at Birkenau.

The recently erected tablets, written in three languages (English, Polish, and Hebrew), immediately contextualize the memorial space as a place of ethnic terror and death. In the current climate of Holocaust memorialization, Auschwitz thus functions as a museum to Jewish genocide, a war memorial to political prisoners and resistance activists, and a cemetery for the hundreds and thousands of inmates who died there.

Within these multiple frames of remembrance Auschwitz has emerged as a well-maintained memorial park. Inside the park lies a vast expanse of refurbished buildings that include the original prison and barracks, the sterilization and experimental centers, a brothel, a hospital, and the storage facilities that housed canisters of lethal gas.[5] In visiting Auschwitz on a spring or summer day, the impression of the former death camp is that of a tranquil tree-lined village whose terrible history remains concealed within the sanitized brick structures that house the museum collections. Today five former cell blocks of the camp comprise what the state defines as the "general exhibition" space at Auschwitz I. Taken together these blocks contain installations on the development of the technologies of human extermination (Block 4), the extent of Nazi crimes against humanity (Block 5), the history of the everyday lives of the prisoners (Blocks 6 and 7), and the "death block" and execution center (Block 11). In addition to the general exhibition halls, there are also smaller blocks that contain national installations from diverse countries whose citizens were incarcerated at the camp between 1940 and 1945. Included in these national exhibitions is Block 27 (the Jewish Pavilion), an exhibit that is solely dedicated to the Suffering and Struggle of the Jews who, after 1942, made up the vast majority of the Auschwitz prisoner population. The Jewish Pavilion, for which the state of Israel is responsible, was originally established in 1968.

Starting with the general exhibition space, I conducted my fieldwork primarily in Blocks 4, 5, 6, 7, 11, and 27, many of which are the most frequently visited buildings in the state museum. During numerous visits to these sites, I gathered data on the representation of women in museum photographs, sculptural art, and material artifacts. I took field notes and photographs of the exhibits in each block, the imagery of which became the basis for a content analysis of the various and diverse installations. In total, I analyzed over 200 photographs, ten memorial sculptures, and numerous artifact installations. The analysis of this extensive visual archive indicated that, while women are well represented at Auschwitz, women's memory is constructed primarily through two visual frames: women as mothers, and women as embodied subjects of Nazi atrocities. In the first frame women are recalled through the lens of traditional motherhood and maternal suffering. The second motif, by comparison, focuses on visual narratives of female subjugation, captivity, and violation. Thus, as a site of collective memory, the study of Auschwitz reveals the complex ways in which women's experience is recalled through gendered texts that reify traditional representations of women as either suffering mothers and/or sexual possessions of the perpetrators.

Women as mothers in death-camp narratives

Over a decade ago, Joan Ringelheim, one of the earliest feminist scholars of Holocaust memory, pointed out the absence of gender as a category of remembrance in Holocaust museum culture. As an outspoken critic of the Holocaust Memorial Museum in Washington, DC, Ringelheim maintained that, while various other groups, including prisoners of war and Jehovah's Witnesses, are identified as target populations in the museum installations, women specifically as gendered victims have been largely forgotten in the commemorative re-telling of Jewish genocide. In particular she admonished the museum organizers for ignoring the special burdens that women endured, including "sexual victimization, pregnancy, abortion, childbirth, killing of newborn babies in the camps to save the mothers, the care of the children, and many decisions about separation from children."[6]

In view of Ringelheim's findings on the Holocaust Memorial Museum in Washington, DC, the research on women at Auschwitz suggests that, within this memorial space, the trope of victimized maternity is among the most pervasive themes of Holocaust remembrance at the death-camp site. Previous scholarship on Holocaust memorialization has noted the frequency with which images of the endangered mother and child are used to commemorate Nazi genocide.[7] The most extensive research to date on the role of the mother in Holocaust memory is Judith Tydor Baumel's study of women's representation in Israeli Holocaust memorials.[8] In a fascinating and comprehensive study of figurative Holocaust commemoration, Baumel found that, although there are four gender motifs in Israeli Holocaust culture—women as mothers, virgins, warriors, and weeping elderly victims—it is the image of women as mothers, she argues, that has come to dominate Israeli Holocaust iconography:

> The mother – without a doubt the most common image of women
> in Holocaust memorials. Holding children, protecting toddlers,
> carrying infants, heavily pregnant – all of these images appear
> time and again from the mother defending her child in Rappaport's

Warsaw ghetto monument, to Illana Gur's statue of a mother
holding a child at the entrance to Yad Vashem; from David Olar's
limestone representation at Beit Lochamei Hagetaot of a mother
protecting her children. ... It appears in commissioned monuments
as well as donated ones and is prevalent not only in Israeli Holocaust
memorials but in those found throughout the world.[9]

Baumel's observations on Israeli (and global) Holocaust memorial
culture is consistent with the findings on maternal imagery in European memorials as well. Similar to the Israeli monuments, European sculptures dramatically illustrate, through three-dimensional
figures, the way in which mothers and children suffered under the
Nazi regime.[10] As a trope of memory, the suffering of mothers, their
death and the death of their children, therefore act as a powerful
reminder of a type of human evil that the Holocaust has come to
represent in the collective imagination.

At Auschwitz such narratives are evident both in the photographic archives as well as the sculptural representations that line
the museum halls. Beginning at Block 4, the general exhibition
space portrays the deportation and mass extermination of the Jews.
Within these memorial spaces, Room 1 contains an urn with ashes
of Jewish victims from Birkenau, while Room 2 provides a textual
narrative (in numerous languages, including English) that describes
Auschwitz as the "biggest center for the mass extermination of European Jews." Room 3 consists of large mural-sized photographs that
feature women and children standing at the edge of train tracks and
in small groups as they await selection either for the experimentation centers or the gas chambers at Birkenau. The originals of these
photographs are believed to have been taken by two SS photographers who documented the arrival of Jews from Hungary in 1944.[11]
Among the largest and most prominent of these images is a grainy
black and white picture of rural peasant women, bundled in heavy
overcoats and holding children tightly by the hand. The chimneys of
the crematoria can be seen in the background. A caption beneath the
photograph reads in Polish and English: "Jewish Families in Front of
Crematorium III."

These poignant images of women and children arriving at the camp create a specific kind of gendered memory, one in which the family and especially mothers and children have been targeted for genocide. As the primary visual frame through which the visitor enters Auschwitz, these images thus establish a narrative of the Holocaust that begins with the memory of the Jewish maternal, a trope of remembrance that persists throughout the exhibition spaces and takes on particular meaning in Block 6 where post-Holocaust sculptures use figurative representations to re-create the suffering and starvation of mothers and children at the death camp. The first sculpture, "Mother and Child" (Figure 2), an art piece by Anna Ravnoch-Brzozowska, is carved out of a stone material that resembles unpolished marble. In this sculpture, a mother is seated on what appears to be a concrete slab, her child peeking out from behind her. The heads of both mother and child have been shaved and they are dressed in shapeless prisoner's garb. The chiseled gaze of both figures looks outward toward an unseen fate, their expressions of fear and resignation conveying a sense of anxiousness and foreboding.

Nearby, a bronze set of maternal figures, entitled "Hunger" (Figure 3) and sculpted by Mieczyslaw Stobierski, tells a similar narrative of mothers and children at Auschwitz. In this representation of death-camp deprivation, five naked women are huddled together, their skeletal and undernourished bodies pressed against one another for warmth and comfort. An empty plate sits in front of one of the women; behind her, the head of a child is barely visible as she lies in her mother's arms. The most striking figure of the bronze quintet is that of the female inmate whose blanket has fallen from her shoulders to reveal an emaciated breast protruding from a skeletal rib cage. This image in particular resonates with an authenticity that is reflected in the emaciated nakedness of the maternal body, an image that is consistent with the photographic installations of starved and desperate camp inmates.

Similar to the memorials and museums described by Baumel, these heart-rending images of helpless mothers and children at Auschwitz contribute to the construction of an empathic-based collective memory that facilitates an emotional connection to the

2. "Mother and Child".

horrors of the past. The prevalence of maternal imagery in both photographic and figurative representations at Auschwitz thus functions as a narrative of gendered violence that, in its universalizing symbolism, creates an especially strong emotive context through which to view and remember the history of Nazi crimes against humanity. At the same time, however, the trope of suffering motherhood also fosters a persistent memory of Jewish genocide in which the remembrance of Jewish men's emasculation remains a subtext of Holocaust memorialization. As other studies of genocide suggest, cultural narratives of the violation and death of racialized women are frequently framed within the context of gendered constructions of ethnicity and race.[12] Thus the suffering and extermination of Jewish women, as it is represented in Holocaust art and photography, conveys a memory of men as well, one in which their absence from the scenes of genocide and their inability to protect the maternal victim calls into question the masculinity of Jewish men.

According to Susan Gubar, one response to the inability of Jewish fathers to protect women and children from Nazi brutality has been to frame Jewish genocide as "a cataclysmic break in the history of masculinity."[13] Although recent research on survivor narratives has challenged the memory of the absent and non-protective Jewish father,[14] repetitive images of victimized women and children at Auschwitz nonetheless continue to reproduce this gendered memory in the memorialization of mass trauma. While such imagery serves as a powerful reminder of the vulnerability of mothers and children in war and in genocidal histories in particular, they also provide a lens through which to recall an inferior and racialized fatherhood. This cultural construction of contested masculinity lends support to a type of victim blaming in which Jewish men are held accountable for the suffering of Jewish women and children. As a persistent theme of traumatic memory, the evocation of victimized mothers highlights the ineffectuality and assumed cowardice of non-protective fathers, an effect of maternal memory that is further complicated by the over-representation of the female body in exhibits that recall the atrocities and sadism of the Nazi perpetrators.

3. "Hunger".

Embodied memory: women and atrocity remembrance at Auschwitz

Much of the atrocity history at Auschwitz is memorialized in Block 6 (Rooms 4 and 6) where the evidence of systematic starvation and experimentation is commemorated through photographic installations in which the bodies of the tortured and mutilated inmates have been placed on display. It is here where the surgically altered bodies of Jewish and Roma (Gypsy) inmates, mostly children, provide a visual narrative of the pseudo-scientific experiments for which Auschwitz became renowned under the supervision and direction of Josef Mengele. Part of Mengele's project was to document, through photography, the damaged bodies and infected organs of the subject population. To this end, he ordered prison photographers to photograph the bodies of the women, men, and children on whom he had experimented, highlighting the diseased or destroyed body parts that had been affected by sterilization, surgery, and infection. As a result, when the former prisoners returned to Auschwitz to establish a memorial, hundreds of these atrocity photographs were uncovered, many of which hang in the museum today.[15]

Within this graphic and visually explicit exhibition space, a large cavernous hall (Room 4) contains both the images of the experimental subject and evidence of other forms of bodily suffering that were documented by the Soviet authorities when they took charge of the camp after the Germans fled. In discovering the surviving inmate population, Soviet medical personnel photographed the prisoners who, having been barely kept alive, exhibited signs of extreme starvation and malnutrition. Like the Nazi photographers, the Soviets posed their subjects for the purposes of medical interest, thus revealing the damaged and altered physiology of the starved survivors. Although both women and men were systematically starved to death, it is primarily the female body through which this photographic memory of Nazi crimes is represented in the museum installations. Stretching across the full length of the exhibition hall, six different poses of starved female inmates comprise the visual context for the remembrance of this war crime. Enlarged to many times their original size, the pictures have been given their own privileged space as a separate exhibit inside Block 6. One photograph shows a painfully thin woman lying on her back with one leg bent. Her skeletal hand, placed across her abdomen, barely shields her genitals from view. The caption below the photograph reads:

> A Jewish women from Holland. 37 years old. In Auschwitz since October 1944. Before she was put in the camp she weighed 47 kg. At the moment of taking this photograph she weighed 23 kg.

A second wall-sized photograph exposes the emaciated breast and protruding rib cage of another female inmate who has been made to sit upright with knees bent to her chest, her long legs barely concealing the darkened area of her shadowed lower body. The brief narrative for this picture identifies the women as 31 years of age and weighing less than 60 pounds.

Because these photographs, like those taken by the Nazi experimenters, were intended for medical purposes, they function similarly in the museum space, each set of pictures offering a kind of "scientific representation" of the dehumanized embodied subject. As such, these as well as the adjacent exhibitions (of experimental atrocities and starvation) are reminiscent of a prewar European obsession with the racialized and anatomically grotesque "Other."[16] In particular, the atrocity photographs in Block 6 bear an uncanny resemblance to nineteenth-century pseudo-scientific illustrations of racial depravity, gender inferiority, and criminality.[17] Like the nineteenth-century studies of female deviance by the anthropologist Cesare Lombroso,[18] the medical photographs on display at Auschwitz reveal a fascination with the racialized and dehumanized human subject whose body has become the visual text for the recording and remembrance of Nazi sadism and brutality.

Exhibits such as those found in Block 6 thus contribute to a specifically gendered form of Holocaust remembering, one in which violations of women's bodies are at the center of atrocity narratives. This aspect of genocide remembrance is also found in other photographic imagery that features women inmates in various scenes of captivity and submission. Two examples from the photographic displays in the Jewish Pavilion (Block 27) highlight this phenomenon. In one picture, a naked woman, her breasts and genitals clearly visible to the camera, is shown being led to the gas chambers by a female guard. The guard holds a rifle in one hand and the prisoner's arm in the other. As the guard escorts the prisoner toward the gas chamber, neither of the women look at one another. Their eyes are cast downward as the woman is guided toward her death. Perhaps more than any other image in the exhibit, this photograph captures a defining memory of the Holocaust as a genocidal history in which the systematic dehumanization of a people is represented in the imagery of two women, one whose subjugation is made explicit by her nakedness, the other whose power is subtly but dramatically made visible by the uniform she wears and the gun she holds in her hand.

A second photograph in the exhibit similarly places a naked woman prisoner at the center of an outdoor camp scene in which a woman is shown seated on snow-covered ground. The woman, obviously a captive and unable to escape the camera's eye, appears to be looking directly at the photographer. With one hand she shields her left breast from view while with the other arm she conceals her torso and abdomen. Her facial expression looks strangely calm at the moment that she is photographed, her look one of near defiance in the face of yet another invasive act. Because this picture was taken from close range, it is most likely that the photographer was a camp official in charge of the murder of the prisoner. Sybil Milton reports that photographs such as these, of nude women in various camp settings, were often the work of amateur photographers who, "identical with the killers," photographed their victims for their own "private amusement."[19] A careful look at this picture reveals that the woman is surrounded by heavily clad Nazi soldiers, their large and imposing boots encircling and imprisoning her. It is thus the perspective of the perpetrator that frames the memory of this female inmate, creating a visual narrative of sexual domination, captivity, and certain death.

Further, it is significant to note that in the two photographs described above neither of the female subjects appear to be starved or diseased. Rather, the relatively healthy condition of their bodies would suggest that the women had either worked in an area of the camp that provided greater resources for the inmates (possibly a brothel) or that they had only recently arrived at Auschwitz. As an image of gendered memory, therefore, the impression that these photographs convey is one of beauty and sexualized danger. As such, these two images in particular allow for a sexualized reading of the visual text, an effect of atrocity remembrance that, according to Susan Sontag, may "turn an event or person into something that can be possessed."[20] Other scholars, most notably Marianne Hirsch, have pointed out that similar interpretations can be made of children's images in post-Holocaust memory.[21] In her work on visual culture, Hirsch interrogates the way in which the now famous picture of "the boy from Warsaw" has repeatedly been used to convey Nazi terrorism. As Hirsch points out, the frequently reproduced photograph of the young Warsaw boy, his hands held up in surrender to the Nazis, has become a universal symbol of Jewish catastrophe in postwar European culture, his image appearing in documentary films, tourist brochures, as well as television programs. Discussing this phenomenon, as well as the overuse of images of the adolescent Anne Frank, Hirsch describes what she sees as the potentially exploitive and voyeuristic aspect of child-centered memory:

> Culturally, at the end of the twentieth century, the figure of the child is an adult construction, the site of adult fantasy, fear and desire. As recent controversies suggest, our culture has a great deal invested in the child's innocence and vulnerability and, at the same time, in their eroticism and knowledge.[22]

As in the case of children of the Holocaust, the visual memories of violated women can also create a site of fantasy that is further problematized by installations that feature the atrocity artifacts of the former inmates. Shielded by glass walls, these installations house clothing, suitcases, eyeglasses, religious garments, as well as other human remains that were found when the Soviets entered the camp. While visitors to the museum report that these installations are among the most powerful forms of memorialization at Auschwitz,[23] critics of these exhibits have pointed out that these displays may also fetishize the memory of the dead, creating a memorial context in which personal objects of the deceased become the source of devotion and worship. Writing in *The Texture of Memory*, James Young thus concludes:

> At least part of our veneration of ruins and artifacts stems from the nineteenth-century belief that such objects embody the spirit of the people who made and used them. In this view, museum objects are not only remnants of the people they once belonged to, but also traces of the values, ideas, and character of the time. In the subsequent fetishization of artifacts by curators, and of ruins by the "memory tourist," however, we risk mistaking the piece for the whole ... armless sleeves, eyeless lenses, headless caps, footless shoes: victims are known only by their absence, by the moment of their destruction.[24]

In addition to the trend toward fetishization, the human artifacts at Auschwitz also create a gendered memory of disembodied victims, one in which the deceased, rather than marked by their absence, are painfully present in the survival of bodily remains that have come to represent their lost lives. Within Holocaust memorial culture, the most visually compelling and emotionally charged of these artifact installations are those that display the remnants of human hair. Housed apart from the other displays of material culture, the hair exhibit is situated in the same block (Block 4) as the installation on extermination. In this exhibit of gas canisters and photographs of naked women running to the gas chambers, large masses of women's hair are positioned next to bolts of cloth that were made with hair-based fabric.[25]

In comparison with the displays that house eyeglasses, suitcases, shoes, and toys, the remnant hair installations truly fetishize the memory of the dead who are at once both dehumanized and eroticized in this memorial space. Because women's hair is a potent symbol of female sexuality, this relic of the human body, removed and disconnected from the individual, contributes even further to the sexualization of women's memory. As a disembodied artifact, remnant hair, more so than any other relic, transports the observer into the personal horror of the victim whose shaved and burned bodies can more intimately and graphically be imagined in the presence of this surviving relic. Such displays, along with the female-centered atrocity photographs, have resulted in an eroticization of atrocity memory, as the Auschwitz survivor, Karen Goertz, explains:

> People came to me with brothel fantasies and wanted to know if I had been raped. I would say, "no, but they almost killed me," and would go on about racial shame (rassenshande). ... If their interest waned, then I knew that their intimate question served a disingenuous interest. There is, after all, such a thing as concentration camp pornography. The idea of having absolute power over others arouses feelings of pleasure.[26]

Goertz's experience suggests that, as the female body becomes a significant lens through which the worst of Nazi crimes and atrocities are remembered, museums such as Auschwitz may invoke a fascination with the horrors of the past, creating public memory spaces that invite fantasy and an objectification of the female victims. Further, as in the case of the trope of helpless motherhood, the motif of the vulnerable and sexually objectified female inmate tells a counter-story of emasculation that recalls the inability of Jewish men to protect women from rape, bodily humiliation, and invasive photography that had the underpinnings of pornographic intent.

Genocide and the dilemma of women's memory

The analysis of women's memory at Auschwitz illuminates the way in which gender representation at the death-camp museum re-inscribes into public consciousness the bifurcating images of endangered motherhood and sexual captivity. This dichotomy in women's memorialization raises a number of significant questions for the social construction of gendered memories of atrocity and genocidal histories. Among the most significant of these questions is to what extent do these representations contribute to gender stereotypes that only partially document the realities of women's lives under conditions of violence and genocide? In privileging the suffering and helplessness of women, do these representations erase the memory of women's resistance in the face of Nazi terrorism? As the history of the Holocaust has shown, women assumed multiple roles under Nazi oppression, including those that involved overt and covert resistance as well as extreme risk-taking behaviors.[27] Yet such memories, while not entirely ignored, are much less in evidence than the recollections of helplessness and captivity.[28] Like other memories of the Holocaust, the museum at Auschwitz places victimized woman at the center of the atrocity narratives, fostering an emotional connection to the past that is filtered through images of women's powerlessness rather than representations of their heroism.

Further, the overuse of gendered atrocity imagery at Auschwitz raises significant questions concerning privacy and the respectful remembrance of the dead. As Milton reminds us in her discussion of the dissemination of Holocaust film footage, the prisoners in these films neither consented to be photographed nor gave their permission for "their private agony" to become the subject of public viewing.[29] And yet, in the construction of collective memory, it is primarily their victimization that has become the means through which we study, remember, and visualize the genocide of World War II. In addressing this trend in Holocaust culture, Jeffrey Alexander points out:

> such memorializations aim to create structures that dramatize the tragedy of the Holocaust and provide opportunities for contemporaries, now so far removed from the original scene, powerfully to reexperience it. In these efforts, personalization remains an immensely important dramatic vehicle.[30]

When women's bodies are the "dramatic vehicle" through which these catastrophes are conveyed, however, the effects of voyeurism and sexual objectification problematize the emotive and connective value of these norms of atrocity remembrance.

With the late twentieth-century tragedies of Africa and Eastern Europe, this dilemma of Holocaust memorialization has in recent years been expanded to include other sites of genocide. As nations such as Rwanda and Bosnia seek to memorialize and remember their own histories of violence, the questions of gender representation that have been raised here are especially relevant for the construction of museums and memorials to the more recent victims of ethnic, racial, and religious terror. The developing research in this field indicates that many of these countries are already struggling with the tensions of commemorating mass rape and genocide.[31] Timothy Longman and Theoneste Rutagengwa report that a recently established memorial in a Rwandan church recalls the rape of women with the bones of the victims, their legs positioned to show the sexual violence they endured.[32] Such contemporary exhibits suggest that, in calling for better and more accurate recollections of violence against women, feminist as well as other scholars must be wary of promoting visual narratives that portray rape, subjugation, and torture in such a way as to violate the memory of the dead. The challenge for the future is thus to find a balance between truth and exploitation in the representation of women's memory and the realities of human suffering.

Notes to Chapter 2

1. Strzelecka, Irena, "Women," in Y. Gutman and M. Berenbaum (eds), *Anatomy of the Auschwitz Death Camp* (Bloomington: Indiana University Press, 1998), pp. 393–411.

2. In returning to Auschwitz after liberation, the surviving prisoners found most of the buildings still intact. Two years later, many of the camp structures, including the barracks and crematoria, had been dismantled by the local population for use as building materials. For a discussion of the relationship between the town of Oświęcim and the memorial at Auschwitz, see Stelling, Alison, Andrew Charlesworth, Robert Guzik and Michal Paszkowski, "A tale of two institutions: Shaping Oświęcim-Auschwitz," *Geoforum* 39 (2008), pp. 401–3.

3. Struk, Janina, *Photographing the Holocaust* (London: I.B.Tauris, 2004).

4. Young, James, *The Texture of Memory: Holocaust Memorials and Meanings* (New Haven: Yale University Press, 1993).

5. The hospital, brothel, and experimentation blocks, while identified by signage, are closed to visitors. The artifacts from these buildings have been placed in installations in the central exhibit halls.

6. Ringelheim, Joan, "The split between gender and the Holocaust," in D. Ofer and L. Weitzman (eds), *Women and the Holocaust* (New Haven: Yale University Press, 1998), p. 350.

7. Baumel, Judith Tydor, *Double Jeopardy: Gender and the Holocaust* (London: Valentine Mitchell, 1998); Eschebach, Insa, "Engendered oblivion: Commemorating Jewish inmates at the Ravensbrück Memorial," in J.T. Baumel and T. Cohen (eds), *Gender, Place and Memory in the Modern Jewish Experience* (London: Valentine Mitchell, 2003), pp. 126–42; Zelizer, Barbie. "Women in Holocaust photography," in B. Zelizer (ed), *Visual Culture and the Holocaust* (New Jersey: Rutgers University Press, 2001), pp. 247–60.

8. Baumel, *Double Jeopardy: Gender and the Holocaust.*

9. *Ibid.*, p. 214.

10. Eschebach, Insa, "Engendered oblivion: Commemorating Jewish inmates at the Ravensbrück Memorial."

11. The originals of these photographs were found in an album that

was discovered by a prisoner when she was freed from Auschwitz. The album, known as the Lili Jacob album, contained about 200 photographs that, according to the testimony of prison photographers, were taken by SS officers Ernst Hofmann and Bernhardt Walter. For a discussion of the album and the Nazi photographers, see Janina Struk, *Photographing the Holocaust*.

12. Lentin, Ronit (ed), *Gender and Catastrophe* (London, 1997).
13. Gubar, Susan, "Empathic identification in Anne Michael's *Fugitive Pieces*: Masculinity and poetry after Auschwitz," *Signs: A Journal of Women in Culture* 28 (2002), pp. 249–77.
14. Feinstien, Margarete, "Absent fathers, present mothers: Images of parenthood in Holocaust survivor narratives," *Nashim: A Journal of Jewish Women's Studies and Gender Issues* 13 (2007), pp. 155–82.
15. Struk, *Photographing the Holocaust*.
16. Terry, Jennifer and Jacqueline Urla (eds), *Deviant Bodies* (Bloomington: Indiana University Press 1995).
17. Gilman, Sander, *Difference and Pathology: Stereotypes of Sexuality, Race and Madness* (Ithaca: Cornell University Press, 1985); Gilman, Sander, *Freud, Race and Gender* (Princeton: Princeton University Press, 1993); Horn, David, "This norm which is not one: Reading the female body in Lombroso's anthropology."
18. Horn, David, "This norm which is not one: Reading the female body in Lombroso's anthropology," in J. Terry and J. Urla (eds), *Deviant Bodies*.
19. Milton, Sybil, "Sensitive issues about Holocaust films," in A. Grobman and D. Landes (eds), *Genocide: Critical Issues of the Holocaust* (Los Angeles: The Simon Wiesenthal Center, 1983), p. 8.
20. Sontag, Susan, *Regarding the Pain of Others* (New York: Farrar, Straus, Giroux, 2003), p. 81.
21. Hirsch, Marianne, "Projected memory: Holocaust photographs in personal and public fantasy," in M. Bal, J. Crewe, and L. Spitzer (eds), *Acts of Memory: Cultural Recall in the Present* (Hanover, NH: University Press of New England, 1999), pp. 3–23.
22. *Ibid.*, p. 13.
23. Irwin-Zarecka, Iwona, *Frames of Remembrance: The Dynamics of Collective Memory* (New Brunswick: Transaction Publishers, 1994).

24. Young, James, *The Texture of Memory: Holocaust Memorials and Meaning* (New Haven: Yale University Press, 1993), pp. 127, 132.

25. Outside sites such as Majdanek and Auschwitz, the problematic nature of using human hair in Holocaust exhibits has been at the center of controversy, especially in the creation of the Holocaust Memorial Museum in Washington, DC. In place of the real hair, the museum has substituted a photograph of the hair collected at Auschwitz, a decision that honors the wishes of women survivors who objected to the display of remnant hair, in part because such human artifacts may include the remains of murdered loved ones and family members. See Edward Linenthal, *Preserving Memory: The Struggle to Create America's Holocaust Museum* (New York: Columbia University Press, 1996).

26. Goertz, Karen, "Body, trauma, and the rituals of memory: Charlotte Delbo and Ruth Kluger," in J. Epstein and L.H. LefKowitz (eds) *Shaping Losses: Cultural Memory and the Holocaust* (Chicago: University of Illinois Press, 2001), p. 179.

27. Ofer, Dalia and Lenore Weitzman (eds), *Women in the Holocaust* (New Haven: Yale University Press 1998); Rittner, Carol and John Roth (eds), *Women and the Holocaust: Different Voices* (New York: Paragon, 1993).

28. Installations on four Jewish women resistance workers—Regina Saporsztein, Alla Gartner, Ester Weissblum, and Rosa Robota—are included in a larger exhibit on underground activities and resistance at Auschwitz. All four of the women were hung for smuggling explosives to the underground.

29. Milton, Sybil, "Sensitive issues about Holocaust films," p. 9.

30. Alexander, Jeffrey, "On the social construction of moral universes: The Holocaust from war crime to trauma drama," in J. Alexander, R. Eyerman, B. Giesen, N. Smelser, and P. Sztompka (eds), *Cultural Trauma and Collective Memory* (Berkeley: University of California Press, 2004), p. 257.

31. O. Stier and J.S. Landres (eds), *Religion, Violence, Memory and Place* (Bloomington: University of Indiana Press, 2006).

32. Longman, Timothy and Theoneste Rutagengwa, "Religion, memory, and violence in Rwanda," in O. Stier and J.S. Landres (eds), *Religion, Violence, Memory and Place,* pp. 132–49.

CHAPTER 3

RAVENSBRÜCK: THE MEMORIALIZATION OF WOMEN'S SUFFERING AND SURVIVAL

With this chapter, the discussion of gender, collective memory, and Holocaust memorialization shifts from the trauma-filled landscapes of Poland to the sites of terror that have been preserved and maintained in Germany. The existing research on national memory in post-Holocaust German culture is wide ranging and includes explorations into the way in which the history of the Nazi regime has been politicized and socially constructed in postwar German consciousness as well as analyses of Germany's "obsession" with monuments and memorials to the genocide of World War II.[1] While the sheer volume of research on German collective memory is impressive and offers insight into the complex nature of public forms of commemoration, a review of the research reveals the extent to which questions of gender have remained somewhat obscured in this broad field of memory studies. Perhaps the most glaring omission is the absence of an extensive body of scholarship on Ravensbrück. Although this camp holds a particular place in Nazi history as the only concentration camp that was constructed exclusively for women prisoners,[2] critical studies of Holocaust memorialization tend to overlook this site as a significant arena for investigation.

The history of Ravensbrück began when the Nazis opened the first detention center for women prisoners (mostly communists) in 1933 in Moringen. By 1937, a new facility was opened at Lichtenburg in Saxony to accommodate the growing number of women who were being arrested for political and criminal crimes against the state. When Lichtenburg became overcrowded, Ravensbrück was opened in 1938 and 867 women were transferred to the newly constructed camp. By the end of the war, 130,000 women and children, most of whom did not survive, were housed in the overflowing barracks. Among the women sent to Ravensbrück were political activists from various European and Scandinavian countries; German women, including prostitutes, who were designated as criminals; Jehovah's Witnesses; and Jewish, Sinti, and Roma (Gypsy) populations. Initially, the camp was designed and operated as a labor camp, although over time it became a center for medical experimentation and genocide.[3]

The establishment of a memorial at Ravensbrück dates to 1959 when the first museum was constructed in the former prison camp, using artifacts and art that had been donated by survivors. In the 1980s this space was redesigned to house the Exhibition of Nations, which in its early inception included 17 memorial rooms for each of the nationalities, including France, Poland, Denmark, Hungary, and Romania, that comprised the prisoner population. In 1984 a second exhibition space was established in the former SS commander's headquarters that after the war had been occupied by the Soviet army. As one of the few surviving buildings from the war period, the headquarters became the home of "The Anti-Fascist Resistance Fighters Museum."[4] This permanent exhibition was later replaced by two new installations: "Ravensbrück: Topography and History of the Concentration Camp for Women" and "Ravensbrück Women." These newer installations recount the history of the camp from 1939 until the end of the war, including an exhibit on the war crime tribunals in which Ravensbrück guards and officers were tried.

My fieldwork at the camp took place over a series of days in which I visited the museums and the memorial grounds and during which I participated in ritual activities that were performed at the site. Unlike the other camps I studied, most notably Majdanek and Auschwitz, Ravensbrück is unique for its picturesque setting and for the multiple forms of women's representation that inform this site of memorialization. From the numerous and evocative sculptural figures that populate the expansive camp grounds to the looming brick wall that surrounds the camp's perimeter, Ravensbrück stands out as a place of remembrance where motifs of motherhood, survivorship, brutality, and death are framed within an exclusively women's narrative of tragedy, loss, and victimization.

In the discussion that follows, the memorial structures of the camp will be considered within the multiple and sometimes competing frames of memory that reflect the evolution of the site from a Soviet memorial to its current status as a German national monument and a more feminist-oriented state museum. Among the themes that will be explored are representations of maternity and survivorship; visual and textual histories of crimes against women and children; atrocity motifs and the Christianization of memory; the politics of Jewish remembrance; and the importance of rituals at sites of terror. In exploring these diverse themes of memorialization, this chapter illuminates the tensions and complications of creating a memorial space in which women and children are the primary subjects of nation-based trauma narratives.

Maternity, heroism, and survivorship

As a war memorial, Ravensbrück is among the most evocative sites in the European landscape. Chosen as a woman's camp, perhaps for its seclusion, Ravensbrück is situated at the edge of Lake Schwedt near the small town of Fürstenberg in northeast Germany. Surrounded by wooded countryside, the road leading to the camp is marked by a Soviet era (1965) bronze sculptural tableau of three women carrying the body of a dead child on a stretcher (Figure 4). The "Muttergruppe" ("Group of Mothers"), designed by Fritz Cremer,[5] depicts the women in prison garb, their closely cropped hair signifying their status as camp inmates. In this re-created scene of death and child loss, each of the three women strikes a dramatically different pose, embodying the motifs of grief, emotional devastation, and maternal strength that have come to characterize women's memory in German

4. "Muttergruppe".

national consciousness.[6]

The first statue in the group, the leading mother figure, stands nearly eight feet tall, her muscular arms reaching out beneath her prison clothing. In one hand she grips the end of the child's stretcher and with the other cradles a surviving daughter who clings desperately to her mother's skirt. As a commanding and dignified presence, the lead figure conveys an idealized image of maternal forbearance. Looking directly out at the road ahead, she wears a grim but determined expression that contrasts sharply with the other two figures who walk behind her, their heads lowered in sorrow. With pathos and anguish, the "Group of Mothers" tells a wartime story of maternal strength and the tragedy of maternal loss, signaling to the visitor that this memorial site, unlike the men's labor camps at Dachau and Sachsenhausen, takes as its starting point the wartime experiences of mothers and children. The inscription that accompanies the sculpture thematically captures both the tragedy of child loss and the trope of women's resistance:

> The sculpture "Group of Mothers" is meant to remind [us] of the many children who suffered in Ravensbrück but also to give expression to the care given these children by women and mothers in the camp. At the same time, the "Group of Mothers" is also a symbol of women's resistance in Ravensbrück to every form of inhumanity. It stands here as a representative of all the women, mothers, and children of the women's concentration camp at Ravensbrück.

In comparison with the starved and immobile mothers depicted in the artistic renderings at Auschwitz, the "Group of Mothers" implies that women's bodies remained strong and muscular under the conditions of incarceration and that in their suffering there was also nobility and the perseverance of the maternal spirit. Though idealized and unrealistically imagined, "The Group of Mothers" offers a strong and empowering entry point to the landscape of women's memory that, in keeping with the early motifs of communist East Germany, presents these women as heroic figures in the fight against fascism.[7]

Once inside the camp, however, a different kind of heroism defines the memorial space. In the stone-covered grounds where the original buildings once stood, immense billboard-sized photographs of elderly women with lined faces and graying hair create a powerful visual field for the commemoration of those women who survived the atrocities of incarceration. At the site of each heroic banner, a short biography identifies the nationality and years of imprisonment of the survivor. As the visitor gazes across the vast expanse of the former camp grounds, the aging faces of these women define the memorial as a place of life as well as death, as a site of women's power as well as victimization. This motif of commemoration is given further visibility in the history museum where gorgeously rendered oil paintings of survivors, now in their 70s and 80s, feature the women's strong hands and piercing eyes.

From the walls of the museum, these elderly heroes of Ravensbrück look back at themselves, seeing young women as yet untouched by the catastrophe of World War II. The gallery of "Ravensbrück Women," 27 biographies of the former inmates, extends across an entire museum wall, showcasing the former prisoners as they looked before the war, some in glamorous poses, others in more modest schoolgirl portraits. Accounts of those who survived contain lengthy texts and pictures of a postwar life that, in their return to "normalcy," suggests a diminution of the past. This type of memorialization, which appears to be somewhat unique to Ravensbrück, presents an almost transcendent view of the survivor, one that, while life affirming, perhaps simplifies and masks the more painful and complicated struggles that survivors faced, even those who, with some success, were able to rebuild their lives. The missing space of memory, the one that lies between incarceration and liberation, must be imagined and found elsewhere at the camp memorial, places where the memory of the victimized women are remembered in installations that re-create, through art and text, the everyday atrocities that informed prison life. My fieldwork at the site thus brought me to the "other" memorial at Ravensbrück, the spaces of memory where crimes especially against women and children were revealed and where the politics of memorialization continued to inform and problematize a memory of the Holocaust and Jewish women's imprisonment at Ravensbrück.

Commemorating brutality: the remembrance of Nazi crimes against women

In recent years and with the burgeoning of feminist critiques of collective memory, the remembrance of crimes against women and children has become a focus for the scholarship on memory and the production of memorials worldwide. Commenting on the absence of Jewish women's memory at the US Holocaust Memorial Museum in Washington, DC, Joan Ringelheim explains the need to name and recognize the particular Nazi atrocities to which women were subject:

> It is not a question of using gender as the defining characteristic for the P.E. [Permanent Exhibition], but rather indicating somewhere, where appropriate (e.g. arrival at Auschwitz) that women were victimized in particular ways. We say that children and elderly were gassed upon arrival. That is hardly accurate—women and children made up a significant population in these first selections, often 60–70 per cent of those gassed. Such a sentence would not have been difficult or changed the P.E. very much. But it would have been important. Gender may not define the Holocaust, but it is not trivial either.[8]

Similarly, other scholars and feminist activists have called for a collective memory of war and genocide that brings into public consciousness, among other gendered catastrophes, the forced sexual slavery of Korean comfort women in Japan, the assaults on women in Bangladesh, and the more recent mass rapes of women in Bosnia and Rwanda.[9] In response to a heightened awareness of the way in which wartime atrocities are gendered, the historical museum at Ravensbrück has included a number of exhibits that recall, through photographs, texts, and documents, the crimes against women and children, including starvation, infanticide, experimentation, and forced sexual labor.

As described in earlier chapters, photographs are frequently the medium through which Nazi atrocities are remembered and repro-duced at sites of terror and memorialization. The memorial at Ravensbrück is among the exceptions to this trend in photographic representation. Although the historical museum contains large mural-sized photographs, these images, which were primarily intended for use as propaganda by the Nazis, for the most part show clean and well-fed women working in neat and tidy factories or well-dressed prisoners working in the camp grounds. One exception to this find-ing is the installation that documents the history of the Uckermark sub-camp, a site that became an extermination camp for sick pris-oners, new mothers, and Jewish inmates. The Uckermark exhibit is distinguished by a photograph of a starved and naked mother and child who were discovered alive when the camp was liberated. The text that accompanies this photograph is a report from a witness to these camp atrocities. The narrative (in German only) describes the roundup of pregnant women at the camp between 1944 and 1945, the birth of their children, and the babies' deaths from starvation just a few days later. The account also recalls the daily roll calls that took place in front of the barracks where the mothers had just given birth.[10] Forced to stand naked for inspection, their newborns in their arms, many of these women were immediately "selected" for trans-port to Uckermark. Just above this narrative, a large grainy black and white photograph shows the corpses that were found at this sub-camp when Soviet troops arrived, linking the death of mothers and babies specifically to a policy of extermination.

In addition to this graphic portrayal, a second set of atrocity photographs shows the scarred and wounded legs of women prison-ers who were subjected to medical experiments that were intended to simulate war wounds. In these experiments, which are described in detail in the exhibit, the women's legs were cut and infected with bacteria or intentionally broken.[11] Perhaps because of the absence of a photographic archive of these crimes, such as that which exists at Auschwitz, the Ravensbrück installation relies mostly on written texts rather than visual imagery to commemorate these atrocities.

The few photographs that are on display are those that were taken as evidence for the Nuremberg trials after the war had ended. These pictures are posed shots in which the women raise their skirts to provide close-up images of their scarred and mutilated limbs.

While both the Uckermark and medical experiment installations date to earlier camp renovations, a more recent exhibit on forced sexual labor at Ravensbrück has added another dimension to the construction of gendered memory at the women's camp. The current exhibit, which is not yet part of the permanent collection, was developed in collaboration with Berlin University of the Arts and a group of University of Vienna students who in 2005 created the first display on sexual labor in the concentration camps.[12] Originally titled "Sex work in the concentration camps," the University of Vienna project was the first museum exhibition to catalog the history of concentration camp brothels and the types of experiments and living conditions that existed within the Nazi system of forced prostitution. Before arriving at Ravensbrück in 2007, the exhibit opened at the "Werkstaetten-und-Kulturhaus" in Vienna on the 60th anniversary of the liberation of the camps and later moved to the Mauthausen concentration camp memorial. Once at Ravensbrück, the title of the exhibit was modified to include the word "forced" which appears before the term, "sex work." This change signaled the importance of coercion as a category of memory and a shift in the representation of prostitution from "voluntary" to a forced form of sexual labor under the Nazis.[13]

The main text of the Ravensbrück exhibit consists of written narratives in multiple languages that provide a historical account of forced sexual labor. The history begins with references to the Nazi laws against prostitution and the modification of these laws to allow brothels to be set up at 10 different camps in Poland, Austria, and Germany where the Ravensbrück women were sent to work. The exhibit describes the rationale for the brothel system, emphasizing the Nazi use of women prostitutes as a reward for elite male prisoners and as a "safeguard" against homosexuality among German soldiers. The narrative includes descriptions of the brothel buildings and the concerns for secrecy among the Nazi officials. The brothels were classified as *Haeftlings-Sonderbauten*, a term that uses the prefix *sonder*, which was otherwise reserved for "killing" buildings such as gas chambers and crematoria. Within this culture of secrecy, experiments were conducted on gay male prisoners who were forced to have sexual relations with women.[14]

The visuals that frame these narratives appear to have been carefully chosen to avoid voyeurism and exploitative imagery. A large map showing the camp brothel system guides the visitor through the exhibit, with surrounding photographs that feature brothel buildings, vouchers for brothel visits, and Nazi officers (including Himmler) touring brothel facilities. These artifacts and pictures are accompanied by written accounts that specifically recall the victimizing aspect of forced prostitution:

> At first women could "volunteer" for work in the prisoners' brothels. The SS promised them that they would be released after six months, but none of these women were ever released. ... Reports from the sick-bay describe the bad physical condition of the women sent back to Ravensbrück from the brothels. According to these reports, the women were subjected to medical experiments relating to the treatment of sexually transmitted diseases and abortions were performed on them. ... Apart from the institutionalized form of sex labor at the camps, sexual exploitation also occurred on a daily basis without the direct interference of the SS. Sexual violence at the camps often took the form of sexual attacks, forced sexual relations or sexual favors as part of the barter system of the camp.

The most poignant of the written material includes accounts that describe the harsh conditions at Sachsenhausen in which women were forced to see 40 men a day at 15-minute intervals. Other narratives describe the death of a young Polish prisoner who, having been forced to work as prostitute, was killed after she became pregnant.

As a path-breaking installation on women's sexual exploitation during times of war, the exhibit represents an important first step in breaking the silence on forced prostitution. At the same time, the installation has yet to address the difficult subjects of ostracism and rejection that the sex workers experienced within the women's concentration camp culture. Accounts of survivors, both written and oral, illuminate the resentment that other prisoners held for the sex workers and the moral judgments that these women endured at Ravensbrück.[15] Despite what is now known about the cruel realities of brothel life, the forced prostitutes were perceived to have received special treatment, at least before being sent to the brothels. This "privileging" of sex work led to a divisiveness among the prisoner population that undermined women's nurturance and tolerance for one another. The isolation and judgment that the workers experienced compounded the terrible working conditions they faced once they were sent to work at other concentration camps. It was only when they returned, sick and dying, that the other prisoners understood or recognized their suffering. This social dynamic, while briefly alluded to in the exhibition, remains somewhat hidden from view and unspoken.

The silence around women prisoners' discriminatory behaviors toward one another reflects a larger pattern of remembrance in which narratives of a harsh and judgmental women's prison culture are rarely included in exhibits on women in concentration camps. When women's relationships are the subject of memory, the tendency has been to highlight themes of bonding and caretaking,[16] motifs that tend to idealize women's basic goodness and strong social skills in lieu of more negative representations of women's behavior under duress. Jack Morrison, a professor of history and an archivist for the Ravensbrück monument, thus describes women prisoners in the following way:

> Whether caused by nature or nurture, women have always been better than men at sharing, not just things, but themselves. Women could and did go to other women and cry on their shoulders, opening up and pouring out their hearts to them. ... There were countless intimate and deep relationships formed at Ravensbrück among women, and for many of them it was their salvation. Without them, they could not have survived, and even with them—given the conditions in the camp—many did not survive.[17]

Although these remembrances of women in concentration camps reflect the best of women's heroism and support for one another, they mask other more painful truths that were also evident in the terrors of camp life where the pressure to survive often led to a complicated and tension-filled social world where competitiveness, cruelty, and antagonism existed alongside nurturance and empathy. The treatment of the forced prostitutes by other prisoners represents one dimension of this more complicated social reality that has yet to be included in the memory of women's incarceration. Where women's cruelty to other women is remembered are in the installations that commemorate the harsh treatment of women prisoners by women guards.

Narratives of cruelty and suffering: the Christianization of Ravensbrück through representations of evil and martyrdom

As pointed out in the previous section, commemoration of crimes against women and children at Ravensbrück rarely includes the visual images of atrocities and subjugation that are found in other memorial spaces. In comparison with Auschwitz, for example, the history of violence and abuse at the women's camp is more frequently captured in the written texts that describe the horrors of camp life and in the restored isolation cells and torture rooms that are on display in the former prison block. In the absence of photography, the most powerful representations of camp atrocities are found in the museum exhibits that display the artwork of the women prisoners. Although much of this original artwork was destroyed by the Nazi guards, some did survive while many other drawings were re-created from memory by surviving women prisoners immediately after the war. Among the artists who were imprisoned at Ravensbrück were France Audoul, Aat Breur, Violette LeCoq, Helen Ernst, Nina Jirsikova, Maria Kiszpanska, and Felicie Mertens.[18] It was these women who documented the atrocities at the camp, their pictures providing a public record of the cruel and tormenting behavior of the guards and Nazi officers.

In stark and unsparing imagery, the prisoners' drawings illustrate the overcrowded barracks, the arduous work details, the daily line-ups, the torture of the victims, and the presence always of death. In consistent and poignant themes of terror, these artistic render-ings convey a sense of threat and evil that permeated the culture of the camp, tropes of memory that are symbolized in the images of death carts and cape-clad women guards who carry whips. Violette LeCoq's drawing "The Way to Heaven" (Figure 5) dramatically illus-trates a typical scene of death and carnage. In this artistic memory, a caped and menacing guard stands before a truck of sick and dying prisoners whose unclothed bodies have been haphazardly thrown together for the journey to the crematorium. LeCoq's rendering of this nightmarish scene records for future generations the memory of a cruel inhumanity that, in its ghoulish symbolism, associates the woman guard with an evil and demonic power, bringing into harsh relief the cultural constructions of women's vengeful and murder-ous nature, as the unmoved guard oversees the destruction of the inmates under her control.

Other drawings feature women beating other women and admin-istering other forms of punishment in prison cells and torture rooms. In these exhibits, the visitor is brought into the camp's world of terror through visual narratives that highlight women's cruel and inhumane behavior toward one another. The displayed artwork thus offers a more nuanced and painful recollection of the gendered nature of Nazi power relations, reminding the viewer that acts of sadism and dehumanization were not only the purview of Nazi men but that under a regime of terror and coercion women too engaged in acts of torture and unimaginable cruelty. Further, it is significant to point out that the caped figure of the Nazi guard, as a symbol of power and death, resonates with Christian iconography, tying the memory of Ravensbrück to images of a satanic and woman-made hell from which the prisoners cannot escape.

In a related but opposing memory that also draws on religious themes and motifs, a number of sculptures in the national memo-rials (The Exhibit of Nations) commemorate the captive prison-ers as saints and martyrs in scenes of sacrifice and death. Among

5. Violette LeCoq, "The Way to Heaven".

these representations, the memorials to the women of Bulgaria, Hungary, Romania, and the former Yugoslavia are the most dramatic and revealing. Calling on traditional Christian themes to commemorate the lives of the prisoners, these national memorials suggests that, despite the secularization of Soviet ideology in these Eastern European countries, the creators of these sculptures turned toward traditional tropes of Christian sacrifice to remember and honor the women victims of the concentration camp.

In the room dedicated to Romania's victims, a beautifully carved marble statue of a single woman prisoner stands in the center of a re-created prison cell (Figure 6). Surrounded by prison bars, the woman sits upright on her knees, her arms wrapped around her body, her face looking upward toward the sky in what appears to be a gesture toward God to whom she looks for salvation. The memorial to the prisoners of the former Yugoslavia similarly contains just one figurative piece, a small wood-carved statue of a woman bound to a tree. Reminiscent of the martyrdom of Joan of Arc, this sculpture invokes the memory of those who were burned at the stake for refusing to relinquish their faith. In the Romanian and Yugoslavian narratives of persecution and solitary death, the allusion to martyrdom brings together the memory of Nazi terror with that of the religious sufferer, re-creating a sacrificial trope that is conveyed in the victimization of the innocent female captive.

By far the most compelling of these religious narratives is found in the memorial to Hungarian women (Figure 7). This room consists of a life-size wooden sculpture of a female figure who is imprisoned by a wall of rusted nails and metal spikes that threaten to pierce her body and rip apart her flesh. To reinforce the violence of the scene, strips of blood-stained wood surround the body of the tortured prisoner. This figurative piece, signified by crucifixion symbolism, is among the most disturbing of the national memorials and, like the other installations, recalls the solitude of the tortured inmate and the sacrifice of Christian martyrs.

Taken together, the parallel representations of a feminized Nazi evil with that of women's martyrdom frame the memory of the Holocaust within a religiously inspired gendered narrative. In the

6. Romanian Memorial.

7. Hungarian Memorial.

opposing motifs of good and evil, each of the female figures—the demon and the martyr—stands alone in her place in Nazi history, as one is remembered for her ungodliness and the other for her sacrifice to God. Within this interpretive framework, the recollections of atrocities at Ravensbrück provide a moral parable in which the archetypes of women's virtue and women's depravity are re-created and re-imagined in the recollections of Nazi crimes against humanity. Reflecting the Christian theological underpinnings of Eastern European culture, these national memorials resonate with a Christian sensibility that is found elsewhere at the Ravensbrück Memorial, most notably at the statue of the Burdened Woman[19] that overlooks Lake Schwedt.

The Burdened Woman sculpture at Ravensbrück is a towering outdoor figurative piece. Placed atop a 50ft-high pedestal, the monument is comprised of two figures, one woman who carries another in her arms (Figure 8). According to Insa Eschebach, sculptures such as these, that tend to valorize Christian themes of maternal sacrifice, are embedded in a German national consciousness that has come to characterize the culture of memorialization:

> the prominence of women and mothers in German commemorative sculpture does not only point to and imply an assertion of national continuity. A second discourse is superimposed on it—the Christian tradition of martyrdom and salvation. Since the eighteenth century, mourning in Christian cemeteries has been almost exclusively represented through figures and images of women. Relatedly, Weimar war memorials increasingly utilized female figures in mourning, holding the dead in their laps.[20]

In the Burdened Woman statue, such themes are conveyed in an image that is reminiscent of Mother Mary carrying the crucified body of her sacrificed son.[21] Originally intended as part of a larger sculptural group that was designed during the 1950s by the artist Will Lamert, the sculpture now stands by itself as a singular monument to the women of Ravensbrück.[22] Known throughout Germany as the "pieta of Ravensbrück,"[23] the Burdened Woman, like the memorials

8. "Burdened Woman".

in the Exhibit of Nations, frames the memory of Ravensbrück within a specifically national/Christian context that problematizes the role of Jewish memory and raises questions concerning the remembrance of Jewish genocide at German sites of terror.[24] This "Christianization" of women's memory at Ravensbrück invokes a religious narrative of suffering in which the persecution of Jewish women remains obscured.

Genocide and the politics of Jewish memory

From the outset, the establishment of a memorial at Ravensbrück excluded the history of Jewish genocide from the memorial texts. Following the Soviet model of World War II commemoration found elsewhere in Eastern Europe, anti-fascism and Soviet liberation tropes were the primary themes around which Ravensbrück was constructed. In this regard, Maoz Azaryahu writes:

> According to the doctrine of anti-fascism, the Nazi past was not a source of shame but a heroic legacy. Constructed as a moral drama, the historical narrative of anti-fascism was based on the dichotomy of victims and perpetrators to emphasize both fascist barbarity and the heroism of resistance. Significantly, the East German narrative did not elaborate on perpetrators (the villains being the capitalists and their "reactionary" allies) and virtually ignored the victims of the racial discrimination policy of the Third Reich. The legacy of resistance highlighted heroes and martyrs, whose courage and sacrifice embodied the moral matrix of the anti-fascist legacy.[25]

While other East German camp memorials such as Buchenwald and Sachsenhausen maintained this anti-fascist narrative until well after reunification, Ravensbrück had already begun to include the commemoration of Jewish victims by 1988. That year the camp was chosen as the site of East Germany's commemoration of the 50th anniversary of Kristallnacht (The Night of Broken Glass), a decision that was made in response to criticism from the United States over the exclusion of Jewish memory from East Germany.[26] Within two years of the 1988 ceremony, a Jewish commemorative stone was added to the camp's memorial garden. A stone for the Sinti and Roma victims was dedicated in 1993. Following these changes, two new memorial rooms, one for Jewish victims and one for the Sinti and Roma prisoners, were added to the Exhibit of Nations.

Reflecting back on her first visit to Ravensbrück before 1990, Rochelle Saidel, the author of *The Jewish Women of Ravensbrück Concentration Camp*, comments on the visible absence of Jewish memory in the national exhibits:

> Arriving at the Ravensbrück Memorial on that day in 1980, I had virtually no information about the existence of Jewish women in the camp. It merely seemed logical that Hitler would use all methods, including this particular women's camp, in his genocidal Final Solution. ... There was no memorial room for Jewish victims because memorialization was portrayed by nationality and not religion, according to the guide. Each nation was given a small room (former prison block cell), and the survivor committee from that nation was responsible for creating its memorial. The Polish exhibit, for example, had a Roman Catholic religious orientation that obliterated the memory of the thousands of Jewish Polish women that had been Ravensbrück prisoners.[27]

When the Jewish memorial was added more than ten years later, Saidel notes that, in comparison with the other rooms, which were designed by individual nations, the construction of the Jewish installation was done by the museum staff, a fact that may account for the marked difference in this exhibit space.[28] Containing none of the figurative pieces that define the Eastern European displays, the Jewish room primarily consists of artifacts—a yellow star, an identity card, and a single woman's shoe—objects that subtly suggest genocide without naming the policy of extermination.

In addition to these representations, documents concerning the presence of Jewish prisoners are also on display in the museum. Dating to the Soviet era, a number of these displays show prison photographs that, along with the picture of the inmates, detail their arrest and incarceration. In one riveting portrait, the memory of a Jewish prisoner is captured in a visual narrative that conveys the criminality of the Jewish inmate. In this installation, a 48-year-old woman, looking well beyond her years, is pictured both in profile and facing forward, her identification number printed across the striped uniform that signifies her status as a criminal. Below her photograph, the catalog includes a series of descriptors (written in German) that record her crime (blackmarketeering), national-ity (Czech), and her arrival in Ravensbrück in 1941. There is also a copy of a card from the camp documents that lists her crime and, in a barely legible German script, the phrase "Nasty Czech Talmud Jewess."[29]

A close reading of this display thus reveals the persistence of anti-Semitic representations that were included in the early construction of the memorial and that today, without explanation or context, remain part of the complicated presentation of Jewish memory within this memorial space.

At the same time, the post-unification changes to Ravensbrück have sought to expose the differential treatment that affected Sinti, Roma, and Jewish prisoners. A 2003 visitors' guide to Ravensbrück, *Through the Eyes of the Survivors,*[30] contains photographs with survivor testimonies that document the sterilization of Sinti and Roma girls and the extermination of Jewish inmates. In this carefully prepared guide, the genocide of Jewish prisoners is recalled through the "eyes" of the surviving political prisoners, as the following account by Rosa Jochmann reveals:

> In the evening, before they were shipped off, me and Helene crept into the Jewish block. It was a farewell beyond description. They didn't know where they were going, because it was the first time that a shipment like that was leaving. But they had an idea. They gave us everything they had, sending greetings to relatives, to their mothers. When we found out that they had been gassed, do you know what happened then? We were unable to put on mourning clothes or hoist a flag of mourning. Nevertheless, the camp went

silent. We didn't arrange that. There was no singing, and speaking
was reduced to the necessary.[31]

This memorial text captures the sense of loss and mourning that
the non-Jewish prisoners felt for the Jewish inmates whose certain
death, including lethal injections with phenylene, had become
common knowledge among the other inmates. Since 2008, with
an increasing trend toward inclusivity both here and at other camp
memorials in Germany, other textual references to the policy of
Jewish extermination have become more visible in the camp's historical narratives. An exhibit on Jewish women prisoners, for example,
now documents the arrival in 1944 and 1945 of more than 20,000
Jewish women from Auschwitz, the Warsaw Ghetto, and other
camps. The text, in English and German, elaborates on the poor
conditions under which these prisoners lived at Ravensbrück and
their massive deaths from sickness, hunger, and the policies of genocide that were carried out at the camp. References to the deportation
of Jewish women from Ravensbrück to Auschwitz are also included:

> On 5 October 1942, 622 Ravensbrück prisoners were transported
> to the women's section of Auschwitz-Birkenau, among them 522
> Jewish women. Himmler had ordered their deportation "so that the
> women's concentration camp at Ravensbrück can become judenfrei
> [free of Jews]."... Around two-thirds of the Jewish women
> deported from Ravensbrück to Auschwitz in October were selected
> and killed upon arrival.

While these innovations demonstrate the continual shift in
commemorative politics that has characterized the reconstruction
and re-conceptualization of memorials/museums throughout
Germany, the numerous and diverse memorial structures at Ravensbrück continue to pose challenges for an open and public discourse
on Jewish genocide. Although the inclusion of memorial stones for
the Sinti, Roma, and Jewish victims is a vast improvement on the
absence of commemorative symbols, these stones, placed in the
memorial garden, are hard to find and are dwarfed by the larger

and more impressive Wall of the Nations where the citizens of each country are recognized with expansive and highly visible identifying markers. Further, the invisibility of Jewish prisoners in particular is evident in other outdoor memorial spaces where the memory of Jewish women has been obscured. Two sites of commemoration will help to illustrate this point.

The first site is the memorial to Rosa Kugelman that resides at the camp's crematorium. Rosa Kugelman was a member of the Jewish resistance in Belgium when she was deported with her young daughter to Ravensbrück in 1943. Soon after arriving at the camp she died from tuberculosis. In memory of her death, a marble stone with her name and photograph has been set into the remaining outside wall near the crematorium. Her photograph, which is superimposed onto the stone's surface, pre-dates her arrest and shows a young woman with thick hair cascading down her shoulders. Although powerful in its simplicity, the memorial tells nothing of Rosa Kugelman's background or prisoner history.[32] The plaque bears only her name and the date of her birth and death. Because this memorial has been placed at the crematorium, the absence of a Jewish narrative is all the more striking and highlights the as yet unresolved issues of Jewish invisibility in German memory.

Similarly, the cultural framing of the statue of the Burdened Woman further illuminates the erasure of "Jewishness" in the memory of the prisoner population. Based on a true event in which Olga Benario-Prestes, a leader on the Jewish Block, carried another woman from the field, the Burdened Woman monument, as discussed earlier, has been reinterpreted through a religious lens that casts this figurative piece as a grieving mother holding a sacrificed child. This interpretation, with its clear Christian overtones, renders inconsequential the religious background of the real-life prisoners on whom the sculpture was based. Benario-Prestes, while memorialized for her heroism in the Jewish room, is never identified at the Lake Schwedt statue and thus her Jewishness remains unknown to the thousands of visitors who visit the shrine each year and for whom the Burdened Woman has become associated with an ideal of Christian maternity. Like Rosa Kugelman, the Jewish identity of Olga Benario-

Prestes remains obscured. In the absence of a Jewish narrative either at the crematorium or at the shrine of the Burdened Woman, the national monument at Ravensbrück relegates the history of Jewish genocide to "ethnic only" spaces, in effect removing the memory of Jewish annihilation from the more public and well-traveled areas of the memorial setting. The overall effect of the Ravensbrück site is thus the marginalization of Jewish memory within a motif of national remembrance that Christianizes images of women's suffering in visual narratives of remembrance and martyrdom.

Crossing national, religious, and ethnic boundaries: ritual remembrance at Ravensbrück

Thus far, this chapter has explored the many and diverse ways in which Ravensbrück, as a distinctly gendered monument, represents the experiences of women and children who were subject to starvation, torture, and death and who, in some cases, were able to survive under the most extreme conditions of cruelty and punishment. Within this analytic framework, issues surrounding atrocity representation, religious motifs, and Jewish visibility and invisibility have been considered for the way in which each of these aspects of commemoration contribute to the creation of a multilayered and at times contentious form of gendered memory. Although the material culture of Ravensbrück—sculptures, art works, artifacts, and buildings—form the primary focus of memory at this national monument, the study of the women's camp would not be complete without a discussion of the significant role that this site plays in ritual remembrance.

Like other sites of terror, the women's camp at Ravensbrück is a place of ritual and mourning. Throughout Eastern and Western Europe, concentration and death-camp memorials offer some of the most powerful examples of the way in which geographies of violence and death have been transformed into sacred spaces. At Mauthausen in Austria, for example, the crematorium and gas chamber serve as spontaneous memorials both to political prisoners as well as to the 6 million Jewish victims of Nazi genocide. In the open ovens of the immaculately maintained crematorium, Jewish memorial candles burn alongside frayed and yellowed pictures of women, men, and children. In an adjacent room, the shower stalls that once served as gas chambers are similarly covered with pictures of the dead. At the entrance to both the crematorium and gas chambers, visitors pray and meditate, often leaving behind scraps of paper on which the words for God or spirit have been written in Hebrew, Spanish, English, and a myriad of other languages. Here and elsewhere in the Holocaust memorial landscape, technologies of genocide have been transformed and redefined as religious spaces, as the sacred and profane are brought together in a spiritual re-consecration of the death-camp site.

At Ravensbrück, this transformation is accomplished in a decidedly different milieu, one that, rather than contextualized by the technologies of war and death, incorporates the natural surroundings of the camp's wartime history. The rituals that take place at Ravensbrück are typically performed at the base of the Burdened Woman statue where the waters of the lake and the forests of the wooded countryside serve as the site of mourning and remembrance. Framed by the statue of the Burdened Woman, this ritual space evokes an almost mystical quality that is both feminized and inspired by the beauty of the natural setting. Within this designated ritual space of women's remembrance, the power of the feminine, both in nature and in the symbol system of the two women prisoners, is pervasive. Whether viewed through the lens of Mariology or through a more secularized frame of women's empowerment, loss, and survival, the statue, together with the waters of Lake Schwedt, creates a space of memory that invokes a more pastoral and peaceful sense of place, even as the terror of Ravensbrück remains close by.

On the day that I arrived at Ravensbrück, my first view of the camp was from a distant spot along the lake's edge where the statue of the Burdened Woman appeared to be enveloped in a mist that was slowly settling over the camp grounds. Leaving the parking area, I followed the path to the shrine that wound past the crematorium, the memorial garden, and a sculpture of a prisoner wrapped in barbed wire, before ending at the foot of the Burdened Woman monument.

As I approached the sculpture, a group of young students were gathered at the base of the memorial. These visitors were Norwegian high-school students who were on their last stop of an eight-day tour of the labor and death camps of Germany and Eastern Europe. My arrival at the camp coincided with the students' performance of a closing ritual that involved three acts of memorialization: the placing of candles at the base of the Burdened Woman shrine, the singing of anti-war songs, and the casting of roses by the young women in the group into the waters of Lake Schwedt where the ashes of the concentration victims lie buried.

On the day that I observed the students' ritual, the songs that were being performed (in English) included Pete Seeger's "Where Have All the Flowers Gone?" and John Lennon's "Imagine," two anti-war classics that conveyed both the sense of loss that the Holocaust engendered and the possibility of hope that, in remembering the past, a different kind of future might be imagined. "Where Have All the Flowers Gone?", a folk ballad that was popularized in the United States in the 1960s, is a soulful reminder of the unending nature of human conflict and the persistence of human warfare, as a stanza from the song conveys:

Where have all the soldiers gone
Long time passing
Where have all the soldiers gone
Long time ago
Where have all the soldiers gone
They've gone to grave yards everyone
When will they ever learn
When will they ever learn

By contrast, Lennon's "Imagine" offers a different kind of message, suggesting that to imagine a world without violence is to create the possibility of peaceful co-existence and an end to the repetitions of the past:

Imagine there's no country
It isn't hard to do
Nothing to kill or die for
And no religion too
Imagine all the people
Living life in peace …

In choosing each of these songs for their closing ritual at Ravens-brück, the Norwegian students pushed the boundaries of memorial-ization beyond a specifically Christian or Jewish victim population. Framed within a 1960s culture of peace and hope, their message reached beyond the history of Nazism, calling for a more global understanding of war and terror. Distinctly secular in nature, the ritual at Ravensbrück situated the horrors of the past within an anti-war discourse that spoke to the possibility of a better and more humane future. The rites of the students thus functioned both as an act of remembrance and as an act of resistance and social change. Seeking an end to war and violence, their commemorative ceremony transcended the politics of national, religious, and ethnic memory, transforming the concentration camp from a site of national terror and religious tension to a memorial where the meaning of the sacred has been re-framed through the language of peace and the social ethics of non-violence. The ritual life of Ravensbrück thus represents a new and emerging phase of Holocaust memorialization in which sites of terror have become places of international mourning where future generations can seek a common understanding of the lessons of the past. In the months following my visit to Ravensbrück, as I continued my work at other field settings, I increasingly became aware that I had witnessed an act of mourning and remembrance that, in its sorrow and youthful openness, had created for a moment in time a place of hope within this vast terrain of genocidal memory.

Notes to Chapter 3

1. Bodemann, Y. Michal (ed), *Jews, Germans, Memory: Reconstructions of Jewish Life in Germany* (Ann Arbor, MI: University of Michigan Press, 1996); Koontz, Claudia, "Between memory and oblivion: Concentration camps in German memory," in J. Gillis (ed), *Commemorations: The Politics of National Identity* (Princeton, NJ: Princeton University Press, 1994), pp. 258–80; Milton, Sybil, *In Fitting Memory: The Art and Politics of Holocaust Memorials* (Detroit: Wayne State University Press, 1991); Olick, Jeffrey K. and Daniel Levy, "Collective memory and cultural constraint: Holocaust myth and rationality in German politics," *American Sociological Review* 62 (1997), pp. 921–36; Young, James, *The Texture of Memory: Holocaust Memorials and Meaning* (New Haven: Yale University Press, 1993).

2. In 1941 a camp for men was also established within the concentration camp. While many of the death and labor camps, such as Auschwitz and Majdanek, housed both men and women, Dachau was exclusively a men's camp while Ravensbrück was originally intended to house only women. Camps such as Buchenwald, Sachsenhausen, and Nurengamme housed women in brutal conditions in satellite camps but their memory has mostly been forgotten in favor of a greater emphasis on men's imprisonment. See Claudia Koontz, "Between memory and oblivion: Concentration camps in German memory," in J. Gillis (ed), *Commemorations: The Politics of National Identity*.

3. Morrison, Jack, *Ravensbrück: Everyday Life in a Women's Concentration Camp 1939–45* (Princeton, NJ: Mark Wiener, 2000).

4. After occupying the camp, the Soviet army destroyed most of the original buildings.

5. Fritz Cremer designed many of the sculptures in the East German camps, including the tableau of 11 survivors at Buchenwald.

6. Eschebach, Insa, "Engendered oblivion: Commemorating Jewish inmates at the Ravensbrück Memorial," in J.T. Baumel and T. Cohen (eds), *Gender, Place and Memory in the Modern Jewish Experience* (London: Valentine Mitchell, 2003), pp. 126–42.

7. Azaryahu, Maoz, "RePlacing memory: The reorientation of

Buchenwald," *Cultural Geographies* 10 (2003), pp. 1–20; Koontz, Claudia, "Between memory and oblivion: Concentration camps in German memory," in J. Gillis (ed), *Commemorations: The Politics of National Identity*.

8. Ringelheim, Joan, "Gender and genocide: A split memory," in R. Lentin (ed), *Gender and Catastrophe* (London: Zed Books, 1997), p 27.

9. Rozario, Santi, "'Disasters' and Bengladeshi women," in R. Lentin (ed), *Gender and Catastrophe* (London: Zed Books, 1997), pp. 255–68; Sancho, Nelia, "The 'Comfort Women' system in Japan during World War II: Asian women as targets of mass rape and sexual slavery by Japan," in R. Lentin (ed), *Gender and Catastrophe*, pp. 144–54; Stiglmayer, Alexandra (ed), *The War Against Women in Bosnia-Herzgovina* (Lincoln, NE: University of Nebraska Press, 1994).

10. The text here and elsewhere in the earlier exhibits is in German. The translation for this text was done by Patrick Greaney.

11. Morrison, Jack, *Ravensbrück: Everyday Life in a Women's Concentration Camp 1939–45*.

12. It should be noted that, with the recent renovations at Dachau, one installation shows a photograph of women being brought to the camp as prostitutes, documenting the use of sex workers at Dachau, although there is no accompanying narrative on the history of forced prostitution under the Nazis.

13. This information was gathered through correspondence with the staff at the Ravensbrück Memorial.

14. The textual references here are gathered from two sources: the museum catalog, *Sex-Zwangsarbeit in NS-Konzentrationslagern: Katalog zur Ausstellung* (Vienna: Die Aussteller-Verein zur Foerderung von Historischen und Kunsthistorischen Ausstellungen, 2006), translated for this chapter by Patrick Greaney; and the English-language text provided by the Ravensbrück Memorial.

15. Herbermann, Nanda, *The Blessed Abyss: Inmate #6582 in Ravensbrück Concentration Camp for Women*, trans H. Baer (Detroit, MI: Wayne State University Press, 2000).

16. Baumel, Judith Tydor, "Women's agency and survival strategies during the Holocaust," *Women's International Forum* 22 (1999), pp. 329–47.

17. Morrison, *Ravensbrück: Everyday Life in a Women's Concentration Camp*

1939–45, p. 310.

18. Herzog, Monika, *Drawings of Ravensbrück ... "hope, which lives in us eternally"* (Gesamthersetllung: Hentrich, 1993); Morrison, *Ravensbrück: Everyday Life in a Women's Concentration Camp 1939–45*.

19. The title of this sculpture in German is "Tragende" and is sometimes translated as "She Who Carries."

20. Eschebach, Insa, "Engendered oblivion: Commemorating Jewish inmates at the Ravensbrück Memorial," in J.T. Baumel and T. Cohen (eds), *Gender, Place and Memory in the Modern Jewish Experience*, p. 130.

21. A similar figurative piece has been constructed in a small and somewhat obscured grove in Hansaring Park in Cologne. This statue, "Mother and Dead Child" by Mari Andriessen, stands next to a memorial to seven victims of the Gestapo and similarly frames the memory of Nazi crimes through the image of a mother holding a dead child in her arms. On a nearby stone plaque, the following words are written: "Let this marker serve as a reminder of Germany's most shameful hour."

22. The artist died before completing the sculptural group. Two of the other figures in the original tableau now stand together in the courtyard that faces the camp's crematorium.

23. Eschebach, Insa, "Engendered oblivion: Commemorating Jewish inmates at the Ravensbrück Memorial," in J.T. Baumel and T. Cohen (eds), *Gender, Place and Memory in the Modern Jewish Experience*, pp. 126–42.

24. Similar issues have been raised at Auschwitz, particularly over the construction of a convent at the site and the placement of crosses on the camp grounds. For an excellent discussion of the Auschwitz controversy, see Zubrzycki, Genevieve, *The Crosses of Auschwitz: Nationalism and Religion in Post Communist Poland* (Chicago: University of Chicago Press, 2006).

25. Azaryahu, Maoz, "RePlacing memory: The reorientation of Buchenwald."

26. Eschebach suggests that the East German government was motivated by a desire to assure economic support from the United States. See Eschebach, Insa, "Engendered oblivion: Commemorating Jewish inmates at the Ravensbrück Memorial," in J.T. Baumel and T. Cohen (eds), *Gender, Place and Memory in the Modern Jewish Experience*, pp. 126–42.

27. Saidel, Rochelle, *The Jewish Women of Ravensbrück Concentration Camp* (Madison, WI: University of Wisconsin Press, 2004), pp. 4–5.

28. *Ibid.*

29. The original signage is in German, translated by Patrick Greaney.

30. Krause-Schmidt, Ursula and Christine Krause (eds), *Through the Eyes of the Survivors: A Guide to Ravensbrück Memorial Museum* (Stuttgart: Lagergemeinschaft Ravensbrück, 2003).

31. Jochmann, Rosa, *Through the Eyes of the Survivors: A Guide to Ravensbrück Memorial Museum*, p. 19.

32. The information on Rosa Kugelman was found in Rochelle Saidel's book *The Jewish Women of Ravensbrück Concentration Camp*. I initially contacted the camp administration concerning the memorial but they had no record of this prisoner or her background. In their correspondence, the staff were very apologetic, stating that, compared to other Nazi labor camps, the records for Ravensbrück are much less complete.

CHAPTER 4

JEWISH MEMORY AND THE EMASCULATION OF THE SACRED: KRISTALLNACHT IN THE GERMAN LANDSCAPE

In the preceding chapters, the analysis of gender and collective memory has centered on the death and labor camps as the primary sites of Holocaust remembrance. In this chapter, the discussion turns from these bounded geographies of Nazi terror to the more urban memoryscapes of Kristallnacht (The Night of Broken Glass) memorialization that have come to characterize Holocaust remembrance in contemporary Germany. As a yearly event, Kristallnacht commemorations began in Germany in the 1950s when surviving Jewish populations, primarily in East Germany, annually recalled the 1938 attacks against synagogues, Jewish-owned businesses, and Jewish citizens. By the late 1970s, with the growing visibility of the Holocaust in German society, Kristallnacht assumed an increasingly important role, having been identified as the tragic turning point in German history, when violence against the Jews became legitimated and sponsored by the Nazi state.[1]

In the 1980s, Kristallnacht commemorations entered into the national and state arenas with the 1988 ceremonies that marked the 50th anniversary of the pogroms. At the urging of both Jewish and Christian groups, the parliaments in East and West Germany held commemorative ceremonies that year, signaling a new era of German memory in which government officials publicly and actively took part in the memorialization of the 1938 violence. Since the 50th anniversary, the importance of the 1988 ceremonies has been the subject of numerous studies of Holocaust memory. Of particular significance is the role that these ceremonies assumed in framing the memory of Jewish genocide for a postwar German society. In East Germany, as previously discussed, the 1988 commemoration was held at Ravensbrück and was marked by speeches from government officials and members of the East German Jewish community, each of whom recalled the events of November 9, 1938, through the history of Jewish suffering. By comparison, West Germany's ceremony took on a very different tone and national character. In West Germany, the ceremony was distinguished by only one speech, that of Philipp Jenninger, the president of the West German parliament.[2] Speaking as a representative of the West German government, Jenninger, rather than address the tragedy of the German Jews, spoke instead of the culpability of the German citizens:

> Today we have come together in the Bundestag ... because not the victims, but we [sic] in whose midst the crimes took place have to remember and account for what we did; because we Germans want to come to an understanding of our past and of its lessons for our present and future politics.[3]

In a further elaboration of the past, Jenninger referred to the situation in Germany during the 1930s that led to the rise of Nazism, pointing out how the difficulties of the time contributed to the nation's support for Hitler. In situating Kristallnacht within the context of Germany's troubled political and social history, Jenninger's remarks created an upset in the Bundestag where his comments were interpreted as a justification for Nazi crimes. Within a few days of the Kristallnacht ceremony, Jenninger was forced to resign. In the wake of what came to be known as the "Jenninger Affair," future commemorations were framed through a lens of Jewish suffering that avoided, whenever possible, any reference to the actions of the Germans that may have led to the promulgation of anti-Semitic violence.[4]

Since 1989, the year of German unification, Kristallnacht has become among the most significant forms of Holocaust remembrance in contemporary Germany. Each year on November 9, major ceremonies throughout the country openly and publicly mourn the loss of the nation's Jewish population.[5] During these solemn and mournful events, rabbis and leaders of the German Jewish community join with government officials in acknowledging the death and tragedy of the German Jews, although, mindful of the Jenninger debacle, little is said about the social and political conditions under which the crimes were perpetrated. In keeping with this memorial stance, Germany has also produced a plethora of Kristallnacht memorials at sites of violence where Jewish property was destroyed. These memorials take the shape of monuments, sculptures, and restored buildings that are intended to honor and remember the "other victims" of the Night of Broken Glass—the desecrated synagogues and sacred objects that were burned and destroyed during the pogroms. In creating memorials to the lost and violated religious culture, these monuments, like the anniversary events, reproduce the trope of victimization that has become central to Kristallnacht memory, bringing into public consciousness the desecration of the sacred in the memory of Nazi terror.

While a significant number of studies have addressed the development of German Holocaust memorials more broadly,[6] very little of this research focuses specifically on the destroyed synagogue as a separate and distinct memorial site. The goal of this chapter therefore is to examine the role that the synagogue and Jewish sacred objects play in the frames of remembrance that Kristallnacht engenders in contemporary German society. Through an exploration into the representations of synagogue violence at sites of Kristallnacht terror, this chapter illuminates the way in which religious symbolism and sacred spaces have become a significant arena for commemorating the Holocaust in postwar German culture. Further, through an analysis of the imagery and visual narratives of the synagogue memorial sites, the chapter examines the way in which Kristallnacht monuments contribute to the feminization of Jewish religious memory in Germany and the promulgation of motifs of Jewish emasculation in Holocaust remembrance.

Topographies of religious terror: the destroyed synagogue in German national memory

Throughout the modern German landscape, evidence of remnant, destroyed, and rebuilt synagogues offer a constant reminder of Germany's once diverse and flourishing Jewish religious communities. A national guide to "Jewish Germany" lists close to 150 Jewish cultural sites that have been identified by the German government as places of interest that recall Germany's rich and tragic Jewish past.[7] Among these sites are ruins, monuments, and restored synagogues that memorialize the events that took place on November 9 and 10, 1938. These sites, which are found in large cities, small towns, villages, and cemeteries, preserve a memory both of a Jewish past and of the violence of Jewish loss. In conducting my research on Kristallnacht memorialization, I did fieldwork at 50 of these sites, including memorials in four major cities (Berlin, Frankfurt, Cologne, and Hamburg), two mid-sized urban areas (Aachen and Essen), and a number of smaller cites and towns (Friedberg, Spyers, and Worms). The memorials I studied at these diverse sites ranged from small monuments and public sculptures to medieval ruins and Jewish exhibits at state and city museums.[8]

A survey of the diverse and varied Kristallnacht monuments and memorial spaces reveal a number of significant findings on the role and function of Jewish religious memory in German national consciousness. The analysis of data indicate that three predominant themes of Holocaust remembrance appear to define the landscape of synagogue commemoration. These defining themes, which parallel Holocaust memorialization more generally, include the memory of absence, the memory of terror and atrocity, and the memory of death. At the center of each of these motifs representations of violence focus on the synagogue and Jewish ritual objects as the victims of Nazi terror.

The absent synagogue in German national memory

The theme of absence as a trope of Jewish memory in Germany was first identified by James Young in *The Texture of Memory*.[9] In this work, Young begins his analysis of Holocaust memory with a discussion of the "Skulptur Projekte 87," the monument to the "missing Jews of Münster" that was originally installed in front of that city's historic palace and then later demolished and rebuilt in Hamburg where it remains today.[10] Young points out that part of the significance of this monument is the unique place it holds as one of the few national reminders of the absent Jews of Germany. By comparison, the memorials to the missing synagogue are numerous and inhabit multiple sites of memory in a vast array of cities and towns, creating visual markers with street signs, sculptures, vacant spaces, and stone monuments that commemorate the absence of the destroyed buildings.

Two significant examples of this phenomenon are the memorials in the cities of Aachen and Friedberg, each of which offers a different but compelling representation of the memory of the missing synagogue in contemporary German society. As a public space of remembrance, the memorial in Aachen is illustrative of monuments that recall the events of November 9 through the imagery of religious iconography and broken glass. In a large square that is adjacent to the city's main shopping area stands a 12ft-high glass sculpture in the shape of a Jewish star. This monument was built on the site of the original synagogue and until recently stood alone in a city square that now houses a new and modern synagogue. The new synagogue, which was constructed directly across from the monument, serves a growing Jewish community that resides in Aachen. The newly constructed building has been designed with a set of narrow windows that look out onto the Star of David memorial, creating a visual space in which the fractured crystal imagery of the monument is reflected in the window panes of the modern synagogue structure.

As a place of commemoration, the Aachen synagogue square is a unique example of Kristallnacht memorialization that, through both monument culture and synagogue re-creation, brings together the memory of the destroyed synagogue with a contemporary signifier of a living German Jewish community. In contrast to this form of remembrance, in which monuments and buildings form the nexus of Jewish memory, the memorial in Friedberg is defined by emptiness and the absence of structural representations of the former synagogue. In this small city, where few Jews currently reside, the memorial to the missing synagogue is signified by an empty space where the synagogue once stood. Bordered on one side by the remains of the original synagogue wall and on the other side by postwar houses and apartment buildings, the vacant gated park contains a marker bearing the Star of David. At the approximate place where the Ark of the synagogue had been located, a sketch of a Torah has been drawn into cement, symbolizing both the absent building and the missing sacred object.

The vacant landscape of the Friedberg memorial park offers a different type of remembrance than that which is found in Aachen. In comparison with Aachen's synagogue square, Friedberg's public memory is one of absence and desertion, a theme of Holocaust remembrance that is discussed by Ulrich Baer in an important essay on Holocaust photography and the landscape tradition.[11] In this work, Baer analyzes two photographs of Holocaust memory, each of which reveals the empty landscapes of the former concentration camps at Sobibor and Ohrdruf. According to Baer, rather than convey the images of ruins and remnant buildings, these photographic landscapes rely on the aesthetics of place to convey the memory of historical trauma, "pulling the viewer into a setting" of traumatic histories that is invoked through the memory of desertion and abandonment.[12] Similarly, the memorial in Friedberg "pulls" the visitor into the space of the missing synagogue, a vacant urban landscape that is a small but evocative reminder of Jewish loss and cultural destruction.

On the street adjacent to the memorial park, a surviving fifteenth-century *mikveh* (ritual bath) has been re-opened as a tourist site. The entry to the *mikveh* contains photographs of the interior of the former synagogue and of the rabbis and congregants who worshipped there before the war. Across the street from the ritual bath, a prewar rundown building features photographs of the burning synagogue that were taken on the night of November 9. In contrast to a memory of the "void" contained within the empty park space, the photographic displays of the former congregants, and especially of the decimated synagogue, call to mind the genocide of the war period and the atrocities that marked the Nazi regime. In particular, the image of the burning synagogue creates a collective memory of terror and annihilation that is conveyed through the visual narrative of fiery destruction and charred ruins.

Remembering terror: the burned synagogue as Jewish victim

Among the most frequently reproduced symbols of Nazi terror in contemporary German remembrance is the image of the burned and ruined synagogue. In these memory frames, the human element of violence has been erased, with neither the perpetrators nor the Jewish victims visible or present in the photographic representations of the pogroms. Within the visual narratives of Kristallnacht, it is not the Jews but the religious buildings and sacred objects that are at the center of atrocity remembrance. In Friedberg, as described above, the photographs of the burning synagogue are displayed in a visual exhibit of six images, each of which highlights the synagogue at various stages of destruction. In the first photograph, the building is shown soon after the synagogue was set on fire. The next four pictures capture the spread of flames and the increasing demise of the building. Finally, in the last photograph, the image of smoldering ruins brings the visual narrative to a close.

Photographs such as these, which graphically re-create the destruction of November 9, have become commonplace in museums and memorials throughout the country. At the concentration camp museum at Sachsenhausen, for example, attacks against German synagogues are at the center of a large exhibit on Kristallnacht which includes surviving ritual objects, such as Menorahs, that were saved from the burning buildings. Within this installation, a 1938 newsreel of the attack on a large urban synagogue is shown continuously in a televised display that illuminates the surrounding walls with moving pictures of a sky alight with fire as the buildings go up in flames. In this film footage, the words "Die Synagoge" have been superimposed across the images of the burning buildings, making it unmistakably clear that it is a place of Jewish worship that has been attacked. In conjunction with the photographic archive and the newsreel footage, other installations feature the charred remains of ravaged, burned, and spoiled Torah scrolls—ritual objects that, because of their symbolic as well as sacred meaning, were the frequent targets of violence and desecration during the November 9 pogroms. It is these installations, at Sachsenhausen and elsewhere throughout Germany, that place the focus of atrocity remembrance on the body of the scriptures, conveying the memory of genocide through religious imagery and artifacts that connect the horror of the Holocaust to the annihilation of the sacred.

Atrocity memory and the desecrated Torah

Within the existing research on Holocaust memorialization, a number of scholars have examined the use of atrocity images in the commemoration of Jewish genocide.[13] As discussed in Chapters 1 and 2, much of this imagery takes as its subject the Jewish female body as the site of atrocity remembrance. In Germany, a similar pattern of commemoration can be found in the representations of the violated Torah. As the single most significant artifact of Jewish observance, ritual, and theology, the sacred scrolls are a powerful symbol both of the Jewish religion and of the scriptures that bind the Jewish community to God. Thus, their place both in Jewish memory and in German commemoration has grown in importance with the development of Kristallnacht memorialization.

With the recent proliferation of Kristallnacht memorials in Germany, the damaged Torah has assumed a privileged place in German national memory, as evidenced by the city museum of Cologne. In recent years, the central hall of this historical museum has been redesigned to include two sections on Cologne's Jewish history: the flourishing of religious culture in the eighteenth and nineteenth centuries and the events of Kristallnacht. The installations that focus on pre-twentieth-century Jewish life re-create visual narratives of imagined Jewish families at holiday celebrations or lighting Sabbath candles. These mural-sized installations are enhanced by surrounding displays that feature eighteenth- and nineteenth-century religious garments, Kiddush cups, and Sabbath candlesticks. With the shift to the twentieth century, the museum narratives of "ordinary" Jewish life disappear. In their place are textual references to the 1938 pogroms that are framed by newspaper accounts, including photographic images, of the events of November 9. The only ritual objects in this part of the exhibit are the charred remains of badly damaged Torah scrolls that were salvaged from Cologne's prewar synagogues. Preserved under glass, these ruined artifacts are identified as remnants of the Kristallnacht attacks that, because of their damaged condition, serve as representations of Nazi atrocities. Without reference to the deportations and genocide that followed the pogroms, the museum's history of Jewish genocide is framed through the imagery of a violated and tattered Torah.

In the medieval city of Worms, the memory of the absent Jews is similarly commemorated by the juxtaposition of pre-twentieth-century Jewish life with the events of 1938. Unlike Cologne, however, the city of Worms has chosen to create a separate museum space for the remembrance of Worms's former Jewish community. Housed in a small building in the old Jewish section of the city, the museum sits on the grounds of a restored medieval synagogue. While a major portion of the museum exhibit highlights pre-modern Jewish culture (a finding that will be further elaborated in Chapter 5), a small display is dedicated to the events of 1938 and the destruction of the nearby synagogue. In keeping with the pattern of representation that characterized Cologne's memorial to Kristallnacht, ruins of yellowed and scorched Torah scrolls form the centerpiece of the Worms exhibit. A poem in English entitled "Elegy for the Victims of the Holocaust of Worms" accompanies the exhibit and identifies the scrolls as the "survivors" of the former Jewish community:

We are the remnants, unraveled and torn
From the fabric once sturdy, a proud congregation
We, the survivors returned here to mourn
Those others, returned here to mourn ...

As a national memory of Nazi terror, atrocities against the Torah have also been memorialized in public monuments and sculptures. Perhaps the most visible of these memorials is the monument to the former Oberstrasse synagogue in Hamburg. In front of the rebuilt synagogue (now a performance hall), an artistic rendering of the destruction of November 9 has been re-created in a sculpture of a ransacked sacred Ark whose torn curtains are open to reveal the remnants of badly damaged scriptures (Figure 9). This graphic representation of the victimized Ark and Torah powerfully embeds the scene of the synagogue massacre into public memory, memorializing an atrocity against the sacred amidst the renovated homes and professional offices on this busy urban thoroughfare. Distinguished by images of violence and desecration, the Hamburg monument conveys, through Kristallnacht remembrance, a memory of genocide that is symbolized by the violation and death of the synagogue and its ritual objects.

Death and the cemetery in Kristallnacht remembrance

As sites of memory, Jewish cemeteries in Europe have become especially important places of memorialization.[14] The much photographed and well-preserved Jewish cemetery in the old Jewish quarter of Prague is among the most well-known examples of Holocaust memorialization in which the Jewish graveyard has been transformed from religious ground to public memorial space. Because of the 1938 pogroms, German cemeteries, the majority of which were destroyed, rarely replicate the type of graveyard memorialization that exists in Prague. Nonetheless, a number of German Jewish cemeteries have been designated as Holocaust memorials, either because of their vacant landscapes or because of the rare survival of Jewish

9. Synagogue Memorial, Hamburg.

gravestones. With the advent of Kristallnacht commemoration these cemetery grounds have in recent years become places of mourning and remembrance for the lost synagogue, creating a collective memory in which the death of 6 million Jews is recalled along with the loss of the sacred. The memorial to the Bornplatz synagogue in Frankfurt is a good illustration of this phenomenon.

Situated in the center of the city, the site consists of an open grass-filled space where the former synagogue and graveyard were located in prewar Germany. In place of the missing building and gravestones, a small tree orchard has been planted in memory of their destruction. Surrounding this tree-filled landscape is a stone wall that bears the names of the 11,000 Frankfurt Jews who died during the Holocaust. Through a mnemonic of death that incorporates both the loss of humanity and the loss of the synagogue, the Frankfurt site performs two memorial functions, recalling both the extermination of the Jews and the death of the sacred. The Frankfurt cemetery is thus a place of public memory where the annihilation of a religious culture is simultaneously remembered with the genocide of the Jewish people.

Similarly, the Jewish cemetery in Cologne brings together the recollection of the murdered Jews with the death of the defiled synagogue. In comparison with the urban-centered Frankfurt memorial, the Cologne cemetery is situated on the outskirts of the city in a large memorial park that survived the 1938 attacks. Accordingly, the Cologne cemetery is itself a memorial to the absent Jewish community whose graves date from the medieval period to 1940. During the 1960s a Holocaust memorial was built at the entrance to the park. The 20ft-high monument consists of a single stone column that is inscribed with the Star of David. Three memorial plaques, two in bronze and one in stone, commemorate both the loss of Cologne's Jews as well as the annihilation of the larger European Jewish community.

A few feet from this spare and unadorned monument stands a second memorial that is more modern in concept and execution. The newer memorial, a 1978 monument to Kristallnacht, incorporates three distinct religious symbols: a two-tier metal composition of

multiple Stars of David, a 4ft-high Menorah, and a sculpture of unraveled, torn, and unprotected Torah scrolls that lie against a ruined
synagogue wall (Figure 10). The Kristallnacht monument commem-
orates both the night of violence as well as the memory of a ravaged
Torah that was buried in the Cologne cemetery during the attacks.
Compared with the more abstract and less visually graphic Holocaust
memorial, the Kristallnacht monument infuses the memory of loss
with a powerful three-dimensional representation of the body of the
"murdered" scriptures. The allusion to the Torah's death and burial
is unmistakable; the memorial is itself a grave site where visitors
enact rituals of mourning, placing stones on the marbled surface of
the Torah's grave. Thus this monument, revered as the burial ground
for the Torah, invites mourners to remember the lost sacred object in
much the same way that a deceased member of the Jewish community would be mourned. In this pattern of monumentalization, the
death of the scrolls has replaced the death of the Jews as the primary
frame for recalling the genocide of World War II.

Kristallnacht remembrance and the emasculation of the Jewish sacred

In placing the findings of this chapter within the larger frame of
Holocaust studies, varied interpretations of the meaning of Kristallnacht commemoration in Germany have been put forward by a
diverse group of scholars. In his work on Kristallnacht commemoration, Y. Michal Bodemann has argued that the focus on Kristallnacht is an outgrowth of the "theater of collective memory" whereby
ceremonies on November 9, especially at synagogue sites, provide a
forum for clergy and politicians to publicly express their guilt over
the death of German Jews.[15] Jeffrey Olick and Daniel Levy, on the
other hand, have argued that Kristallnacht ceremonies, among other
forms of commemoration, lend support to government narratives
that attribute the rise of Nazism to a small but powerful minority of
anti-Semites, thus obscuring the extent to which anti-Jewish racism
informed German culture.[16] Finally, Elisabeth Domansky argues that

10. Synagogue Memorial, Cologne Cemetery.

11. Synagoga, Trier Cathedral.

highlighting the events of Kristallnacht allows Germans to simultaneously remember and "forget" the Holocaust:

> As the crimes of that night were committed by organized National Socialists while other Germans were bystanders and on-lookers, it became possible for West Germans to think of their main failure as a terrible "indifference." It has yet to be remembered that Germans in the Third Reich were not only indifferent to the fate of the Jews, but they were involved in large numbers in segregating the Jews from German society and in carrying out the Holocaust.[17]

In keeping with Domansky's observation, the research findings of this chapter suggest that the proliferation of Kristallnacht memorials further distances the memory of genocide from German national consciousness. As the loss of the synagogue has become the predominant representation of German violence, both in public spaces and in many of the city and state museums, attacks on a religion rather than on its people have become the primary frame through which the horrors of the Nazi regime are remembered. While all of the motifs of genocide are present in these monuments and installations—absence, terror, and death—it is not the Jews or the Jewish body that is the subject of commemoration but the emblems of religious culture and the symbol systems that signify Jewish worship and observance. Thus, as Olick and Levy suggest, the Holocaust can be re-framed as a period of violent anti-Semitism rather than as an epoch of racial genocide.[18]

Interpreting the findings of the research through the lens of German national memory thus confirms and further establishes the way in which Kristallnacht remembrance serves to preserve German identity by masking the more terrible history of Jewish death and murder. While this reading of these monuments offers valuable insights into the politics of German memory, the data on Kristallnacht commemoration also illuminate the way in which religious symbolism has become part of Holocaust memorialization in German culture and how the representation of this symbolism further problematizes the narratives of contested masculinity in Holocaust remembrance. In Bodemann's critique of Kristallnacht commemoration, he maintains that the pogroms are recalled by three tropes of memory that are disseminated in the photographic representations of Nazi violence: the burning synagogue, the ruined storefront, and, most significantly, the image of non-resistant Jewish men being led to deportation centers. Bodemann asserts that it is this last representation, the Jew as the passive female stereotype (helpless and silent), that is the most damaging of these commemorative narratives.[19]

Building on Bodemann's observations, it could be argued that the proliferation of monuments to the destroyed and spoiled synagogue contributes further to a memory of emasculation that is linked to the humiliation of the Jewish sacred. Because the synagogue and especially the Torah represent the Holy in Jewish religious iconography, imagery of their violent desecration carries with it the imprint of an emasculated God figure. In representing the Torah, the Holy Ark, and the synagogue as "Jewish" victims of the Nazis, Kristallnacht memorials in effect anthropomorphize the sacred, creating a memory of genocide in which the suffering of the divine is remembered through the lens of profanation and humiliation. This humanizing frame of sacred Jewish memory, while fostering an empathy for the ruined buildings and violated relics, calls to mind an earlier period of German anti-Semitism in which the synagogue was depicted as a defeated and vanquished woman.

During this medieval period of intensive Christianization, the triumph of Christianity over Judaism was symbolized by the image of Synagoga, a humiliated female figure whose portrait and memory has been preserved in manuscripts, stained-glass windows, and on the edifices of churches in Cologne, Trier, Worms, and Speyer.[20] In this rendering of the Jewish sacred, the disempowered and weakened synagogue is represented by a diverse set of symbols that portray Synagoga as blindfolded, her crown toppling from her head as she holds the broken tablets of Jewish law in one hand and a broken staff in the other (Figure 11). In these depictions, the blindfold represents the Jews' blindness to the divinity of Christ, and the broken tablets a repudiation of Jewish law.[21] Frequently shown in opposition to Ecclesia, the idealized and noble feminized Church figure, the image of the humiliated and ruined Synagoga has been construed within a spirit/flesh dichotomy in which the synagogue, the fallen woman, represents the flesh, while Ecclesia, the virtuous maiden, represents the spirit. In this regard, Sara Lipton concludes:

> Synagoga's contorted posture is indicative of the infirmity and error of the Old Law, just as Ecclesia's upright stance testifies to her righteousness. The former figure's physical decrepitude thus seems to link the deterioration of the flesh to the Jew's degenerate law. Traditional iconographic analysis then construes these Gothic personifications as diametric opposites, and, implicitly, as manifestations of a dualist approach to sacred and profane, spirit and flesh, sense and letter, ostensibly underlying medieval and Christian anti-Judaism.[22]

In expanding on Lipton's gendered reading of the Syngagoga icon, it should be noted that this Christian portrayal of the Jewish sacred shifts the representation of the Jewish divine from a powerful patriarchal God figure to a defeated and ruined female archetype, a shift that has been reproduced in the narratives of Kristallnacht destruction. Within the context of Germanic Christian iconography, the memorials to Kristallnacht can be read as a modern-day parable of the defeat of Jewish law and the disempowerment of the Jewish God. In this twentieth-century narrative of violence against the sacred, the story of Synagoga is retold in the desecration of the Holy Ark and the reviling of the sacred scrolls, suggesting that once again the powerful patriarchal God of Judaism has been humiliated and feminized by a force greater than itself. This reading of the memorials seems particularly relevant for those sculptures that, with great detail and realism, reproduce the scenes of assault and carnage in which the torn curtains of the Holy Ark are left open to reveal the vulnerable and exposed scriptures lying helplessly on their sides. These intensely graphic renderings, reminiscent of the female form, reify the themes of weakness and silent suffering to which Bodemann refers in his analysis of commemorative photography, bringing images of an emasculated sacred into the public framing of the 1938

pogroms. Thus, the monuments to Kristallnacht, in their visualiza-
tion of violence and destruction, both feminize the synagogue and
emasculate the patriarchal God of Jewish law and religious culture.

Finally, within this interpretative framework, it is important to
point out that this analysis of emasculating imagery is further complicated by the multiple functions that these memorials assume both in
German society and within the Jewish community. Because these are
places of Jewish mourning and remembrance, much of the figurative
sculptures that characterize the memorial sites were constructed in
collaboration with Jewish groups who contributed both financially
and conceptually to the creation of Kristallnacht monuments. As
such, the images of the violated Torah and synagogue ruins invoke
a memory of suffering that emerges out of a post-Holocaust Jewish
memory and imagination, even as these images resonate with
earlier anti-Semitic Christian symbol systems. Since the Holocaust,
a number of Jewish theologians have reframed God as a "limited"
divinity who, like the Jews, suffered at the hands of Nazi terror-
ists.[23] When viewed through this lens of post-Holocaust thought, the
imagery of Kristallnacht becomes its own Jewish narrative of divine
sufferance that has its roots in a post-trauma religious culture. This
reading of Kristallnacht iconography implies that, as a result of the
catastrophe of World War II, there has been a convergence of Jewish
and Christian representations of a suffering and victimized Jewish
God, a narrative that, within the larger framework of gender and
Holocaust memorialization, contributes further to the memory of an
emasculated Jewish victimhood.

Notes to Chapter 4

1. Bodemann, Y. Michal (ed), *Jews, Germans, Memory: Reconstructions of Jewish Life in Germany* (Ann Arbor, MI: University of Michigan Press, 1996); Olick, Jeffrey K. and Daniel Levy, "Collective memory and cultural constraint: Holocaust myth and rationality in German politics," *American Sociological Review* 62 (1997), pp. 921–36; Domansky, Elisabeth, "Kristallnacht, the Holocaust and German unity: The meaning of November 9 as an anniversary in Germany," *History and Memory* 4 (1992), pp. 60–93.

2. Bodemann, *Jews, Germans, Memory: Reconstructions of Jewish Life in Germany*; Olick and Levy, "Collective memory and cultural constraint: Holocaust myth and rationality in German politics," pp. 921–36.; Domansky, "Kristallnacht, the Holocaust and German unity: The meaning of November 9 as an anniversary in Germany," pp. 60–93.

3. Domansky, "Kristallnacht, the Holocaust and German unity: The meaning of November 9 as an anniversary in Germany," p. 66.

4. Olick and Levy, "Collective memory and cultural constraint: Holocaust myth and rationality in German politics," pp. 921–36.

5. Since 1989, November 9 has taken on even greater meaning as an important anniversary date in Germany. On that day in 1989, activists began the dismantling of the Berlin Wall.

6. Koshar, Rudy, *From Monuments to Traces: Artifacts of German Memory, 1870–1990* (Berkeley: University of California Press, 2000); Milton, Sybil, *In Fitting Memory: The Art and Politics of Holocaust Memorials* (Detroit: Wayne State University Press, 1991); Wiedmer, Caroline, *The Claims of Memory: Representations of the Holocaust in Contemporary Germany and France* (Ithaca: Cornell University Press, 1999); Young, James, *The Texture of Memory: Holocaust Memorials and Meaning* (New Haven: Yale University Press, 1993).

7. I obtained the list from two sources: the German National Tourist Office, and Lopez, Billie and Peter Hirsch, *A Traveler's Guide to Jewish Germany* (New York: Pelican Publishing Company, 1998).

8. For the purposes of this research only those synagogues that function primarily as museums and memorial sites have been included in the

study. Refurbished in-use synagogues, such as those in Cologne and Berlin, have therefore been excluded.

9. Young, *The Texture of Memory: Holocaust Memorials and Meaning*.

10. *Ibid.*, p. 18.

11. Baer, Ulrich, "To give memory a place: Holocaust photography and landscape tradition," *Representations* 69 (2000), pp. 38–62.

12. *Ibid.*, p. 43.

13. Hirsch, Marianne, "Surviving images: Holocaust photographs and the work of postmemory," in B. Zelizer (ed), *Visual Culture and the Holocaust* (New Jersey: Rutgers University Press, 2000), pp. 215–42; Zelizer, Barbie, "Women in Holocaust photography," in B. Zelizer, *Visual Culture and the Holocaust*, pp. 247–60.

14. Gruber, Ruth, *Virtually Jewish: Reinventing Jewish Culture in Europe* (Berkeley: University of California Press, 2002); Young, *The Texture of Memory: Holocaust Memorials and Meaning*.

15. Bodemann, Y. Michal, "Reconstructions of history: From Jewish memory to nationalized commemoration of Kristallnacht in Germany," in Bodemann, *Jews, Germans, Memory: Reconstructions of Jewish Life in Germany*, p. 209.

16. Olick and Levy, "Collective memory and cultural constraint: Holocaust myth and rationality in German politics," pp. 921–36.

17. Domansky, "Kristallnacht, the Holocaust and German unity: The meaning of November 9 as an anniversary in Germany," p. 75.

18. Olick and Levy, "Collective memory and cultural constraint: Holocaust myth and rationality in German politics," pp. 921–36.

19. Bodemann, "Reconstructions of history: From Jewish memory to nationalized commemoration of Kristallnacht in Germany," in Bodemann, *Jews, Germans, Memory: Reconstuctions of Jewish Life in Germany*, p. 207.

20. It should be noted that the figure of Synagoga is not unique to Germany but is found throughout Europe, including in the cathedrals of France and Italy. See Schreckenberg, Heinz, *The Jews in Christian Art: An Illustrated History* (New York: Continuum, 1996) for an excellent survey of the Synagoga statuary.

21. Schreckenberg, *The Jews in Christian Art: An Illustrated History*.

22. Lipton, Sara, "The Temple is my body: Gender, carnality and

Synagoga," in E. Frojmovic (ed), *Imagining the Self: Imagining the Other* (Boston: Brill, 2002), p 130.

23. Eimer, Colin, "Jewish and Christian suffering," in D. Cohn-Sherbok (ed), *Holocaust Theology: A Reader* (New York: New York University Press, 2002), pp. 135–8; Jacobs, Steven, "Judaism and Christianity After Auschwitz," in S. Jacobs (ed), *Contemporary Jewish Religious Responses to the Shoah* (New York: University Press of America, 1993), pp. 2–21.

CHAPTER 5

GENDER AND REMEMBRANCE: PRE-NINETEENTH-CENTURY JEWS IN EUROPEAN MEMORY

Over a decade ago the historian Diana Pinto initiated a dialogue on the proliferation of "Jewish space" in post-Holocaust Europe.[1] In her analysis, Pinto observed the extent to which European countries are actively engaged in creating memorials, monuments, and museums that incorporate Jewish history and Jewish life in post-Holocaust societies that are often marked by the absence of a living Jewish community. Commenting on this trend, Pinto remarked that "There are in fact few countries in Europe today that do not choose to exploit the phenomenon of 'Jewish space' whether for noble or opportunistic reasons."[2] As Pinto and others such as Ruth Gerber maintain, these spaces are signified by a plethora of mnemonic structures that include reconstructed synagogues and refurbished Jewish neighborhoods.[3] Among the most significant of these reclamation projects are those that re-frame Jewish memory through the lens of pre-nineteenth-century Jewish life and religious practice. This phenomenon is especially evident in the construction and maintenance of public sites that recall the medieval and pre-modern Jews of Europe whose distinct customs and religious ways of life have become the object of curiosity and Jewish remembrance among cultures whose modern Jewish populations have all but disappeared from public view.

In reclaiming the "rich" Jewish heritage of countries such as the

Czech Republic, Poland, Germany, and Lithuania, national projects of public memory have re-created representations of sixteenth-, seventeenth-, and eighteenth-century Jews at prayer, at home, at centers of learning, and at ritual celebrations. These representations are found in city and state museums, at archaeological sites, and in monuments that valorize Jewish scholars and rabbinic leaders. Just as the monuments of Kristallnacht obscure the memory of German Jewish victims, this turn toward medievalism and early modern representations of Jewish life and practice diminishes the memory of modern Jewry within popular and historical European consciousness. In an exploration into this pattern of Holocaust remembrance, this chapter investigates the ways in which contemporary European engagement in pre-nineteenth-century Jewish life freezes Jewish memory in a pre-genocide historiography that simultaneously reifies patriarchal Jewish culture while at the same time contributes further to the feminization (and demonization) of Jewish men in European society. Drawing on fieldwork at diverse historical sites, including tourist centers in Kracow, Prague, Speyer, and Worms, the chapter discusses the representation of the medieval and early modern Jew in national memory and the uses of medieval ritual spaces as sites of Jewish remembrance. Starting with my fieldwork in Josefov, the preserved Jewish quarter of Prague, the analysis of reclaimed Jewish heritage will begin with my experiences as a feminist researcher in the medieval sites of Jewish worship.

Feminist ethnography in men-only spaces

As discussed in the last chapter, the medieval Jewish ghetto in Prague is among the most visited Jewish tourist sites in Eastern Europe, attracting visitors from North America, Europe, Israel, and Asia. On any given day in the former ghetto, the centuries-old narrow streets are jammed with tourists who follow a clearly marked route that leads from one synagogue to another and from the preserved cemetery to the Nazi-inspired museum of salvaged religious relics. As a Jewish ethnographer making my way through the crowded streets and tourist landmarks, I was struck by the desire and longing, especially among European tour groups, for a glimpse into the thir-teenth-century religious lives of a people whose twentieth-century existence was nowhere in evidence. I observed with both fascination and an ethnographer's eye the hundreds of tourists who wandered through synagogue buildings, snapping pictures and filming their newly discovered Jewish surroundings. While sightseers hurriedly moved in and out of the Jewish monuments, I was struck by the pres-ence of another kind of voyeurism, one in which tourists peered into a Jewish world that, although gone for centuries, has come to repre-sent the Jewish people and Jewish culture in a contemporary Euro-pean memoryscape. As I observed the crowds in the narrow ghetto streets, I felt a sense of unease as the tourists jostled one another for a chance to view the unknown and mysterious religious world of a stigmatized and decimated people.

This sense of unease continued to grow and was further informed by the absence of women as subjects of religious memory in these historical spaces. With an emphasis on medieval and pre-modern modes of Jewish worship and religious ways of being, it became pain-fully clear to me that the story of Jewish women as a religious group would not be told, that their memory would reside in the atrocity images and representations at Auschwitz, Majdanek, and Ravensbrück rather than in the cultural frameworks of a distinct and strongly patriarchal Jewish past. This last observation, like the witnessing of images of women's captivity at Auschwitz, at times challenged my ability to sufficiently separate myself from the research setting. It was, after all, my Jewish kinswomen who were "forgotten" and whose outsider status, although acknowledged, was mostly repre-sented in the secluded and frequently walled-off women's section of the surviving synagogues. As a Jewish woman raised in a more egali-tarian religious tradition, I was never more aware of this history and my own complicated relationship to Jewish orthodox practice than during my research at the Old-New thirteenth-century synagogue in Prague.[4]

Most days of the week this ancient stone building, which is described as the oldest surviving synagogue in Europe, is part of the

Jewish-operated ghetto tours. On Saturdays, however, the synagogue is transformed from a tourist site into a place of worship for the small Jewish community that now resides in Prague. My first visit to the site was on a Friday. Along with at least 50 other visitors, I wandered through the first-floor sanctuary, looking into the Aaron Hakodesh (the Holy Ark), as it is labeled in the tourist literature, sitting on the wooden benches where congregants pray, and leafing through the prayer books that line the pews of the sanctuary. I watched as men, women, and children opened and closed the doors to the Ark and ambled through the sacred spaces that were marked by large and imposing stones that adorned the synagogue floor. No one stopped the visitors, including myself, from walking through these sacred areas of the synagogue; my presence as a woman in the sanctuary went unnoticed.

All this changed when I returned to the synagogue the following day to attend Sabbath services. Like the previous day, I entered the building through the main doorway that opened out to the narrow ghetto street. As in my earlier visit, I walked into the sanctuary and started to take my seat on one of the pews that on the day before had been used by hundreds of tourists, Jews and non-Jews alike, as resting places from the arduous tour itineraries. Just as I was removing my coat, a male congregant rushed up to me. Through a number of strong gestures, he indicated that I must leave the sanctuary immediately and go upstairs to the "women's section." Following his directions, I climbed the ancient and unlit stairway at the back of the sanctuary. At the top of the stairs a line of folding chairs was arranged in a single row that faced a thick stone wall through which small openings had been carved to allow a narrow glimpse into the sanctuary below.

With its narrow slits of light and stone edifice, the women's gallery was clearly a thirteenth-century relic of medieval Jewish practice.[5] Taking my seat next to the other women congregants, I strained to hear the chanting of the men below and to see the Torah scrolls that were being taken from the Ark. Within this medieval and archaic setting, it was easy to imagine my women ancestors who, similarly hidden behind stone walls, had in earlier centuries created their own space of ritual connection to Jewish prayer and tradition. What made this imagined memory all the more poignant was the realization that only the day before I had occupied the sacred places of the synagogue from which I was now prohibited. This realization, as well as the sense of alienation that I felt in the women's gallery, led to a complicated set of emotions.

While I recognized the importance of respecting this community's adherence to gender separation, I also felt a sense of sadness at my exclusion from the sanctuary during Sabbath services. Although I had attended religious services in traditional synagogues elsewhere in Europe, where men and women sat separately, it was the juxtaposition of "tourist" and "worshipper" that struck such an emotional chord in Prague, especially in a synagogue that was so laden with meaning and history. While I knew that many postwar European Jews sought to return to the traditions of their ancestors through the practice of orthodoxy, I nevertheless regretted that Jewish women who wished to worship in the Prague sanctuary were prevented from doing so. I am not sure that what I experienced at the Saturday morning services was a feminist response to exclusion or merely a longing to engage all of my senses—sight, sound, and touch—with the sacred relics of a Jewish past and the material culture of a surviving Jewish tradition.

Sitting through the Sabbath rituals in the women's section, my thoughts and observations were thus at times in contention with one another. I saw both the gendered frames of religious space and the remnants of what had once been a thriving Jewish culture in a ravished Eastern European society. Particularly in Prague, I was aware that I was witness to a religious community that was struggling to reclaim its place as a site of Jewish observance in the aftermath of mass extermination. These thoughts stayed with me throughout my fieldwork and at other sites of religious memory. As my research took me from Prague to Krakow and then to Vilnius before returning to Germany, I saw, both with and without a gendered lens, a decimated Jewish culture in the synagogue and cemetery ruins that scarred the European landscape. It was during this period of my research that I also became aware of the numerous national and local attempts, often in collaboration with Jewish groups, to reclaim, restore, and acknowledge the destroyed and spoiled spaces of Eastern Europe's prewar Jewish heritage; and it was these memorial projects that led me to the refurbished Kazimierz district of Krakow and the medieval sites of German Jewish memory.[6]

Polish Jewish memory and the synagogue memorials of Kazimierz

Among the restoration projects of Eastern Europe, the Kazimierz district stands out as an important marker of Jewish heritage in Poland, a country that has yet to resolve national tensions around the genocide of World War II.[7] Remarking on Polish attitudes towards Jewish genocide, the Polish philosopher Leszek Koczanowicz describes Poland's construction of the Holocaust:

> some Polish people say we lost three million people, the same number as Polish Jews. In saying this, the Poles are not quite fair, there were differences: the Nazis killed the Jewish children, while Polish children were able to go through the Nazi lines without being hurt. So there are differences. But still Poles are upset about the playing down of their fate. Poles will say that every Polish family had someone killed by the Germans. ... I don't think we were responsible for the Holocaust. We were not. The Germans killed the Jews. I don't think we should feel guilty for the Holocaust because we didn't do it. But on the other hand, they were killed on our land, so you know, it doesn't matter: guilty or not ... we have to cope with this fact like a thorn in our body.[8]

It is within this cultural milieu that Jewish heritages sites such as Kazimierz began to take shape in Poland beginning in the 1980s. Representing Krakow's small Jewish quarter (which dates to the fourteenth century), the restoration of Kazimierz reflects the initiatives of a diverse group of contributors who became interested in the importance of European Jewish heritage sites both as commercial enterprises and as places of Jewish memory. Among these groups were private entrepreneurs who developed the commercial district, including Jewish shops, restaurants, and tours, the Center for Jewish Culture, Krakow's urban planning agency, and the European Union and World Monuments Funds.[9] Noting the importance that Kazimierz has assumed as a designated "Jewish space" in Poland, a number of scholars have addressed the fascination with "all things Jewish" that is reflected in Kazimierz's yearly Jewish festival and the district's commercialization of Yiddish culture and music for the consumption of tourists and visitors.[10]

With its numerous restored synagogues, the Kazimierz quarter also functions as the center of Jewish heritage tours. Guides to the district highlight the elaborate sixteenth-century Old Synagogue, the smaller and beautifully restored Remu'h Synagogue, the seventeenth-century Isaac Synagogue, and the more progressive and modern nineteenth-century Temple Synagogue that was founded by the Association of Progressive Jews. The majority of these buildings have been restored and although, like the medieval synagogue in Prague, each has a separate section for women worshippers, the open style and decorative nature of the women's galleries traces, through architectural history, the increasing visibility of women in modern Jewish practice. At the same time, the representations of the Jews in this self-consciously reclaimed Jewish space center around the origins of Hasidism in Polish culture and the Hasidic Jewish male as the primary representative of Polish Jewry.

Among the Jews in Eastern Europe, Hasidism flourished in the eighteenth and nineteenth centuries during a time of political oppression and despair. A form of mystical Judaism, Hasidism stresses the presence of God in all living things, a belief system that had particular appeal for the Jews of Poland who hoped to transcend personal suffering through a connection to the sacred. As an exclusively male-centered orthodoxy, the men of the Hasidic communities sought to discover the spark of God within themselves through observance, prayer, and study.[11] While the prewar history of the Jews in Poland was marked by tensions between the Hasidic traditionalists and the more reform-minded religious progressives, the visual culture of Kazimierz re-creates a Jewish memory in which only Hasidic men appear in synagogue displays, in museum exhibits, and on kiosks that announce the Jewish programs of the Kazimierz district. The museum and cultural center at the restored Isaac Synagogue is perhaps the most well known of these commemorative spaces, whose long and difficult history reveals the complicated relationship between Jewish monuments, the church, and the state.

The Isaac Synagogue and the absence of women

Originally built by a Jewish family in 1638, the Baroque-style Isaac Synagogue did not officially open until 1644 when objections over its size and potential threat to its Christian neighbors were finally resolved. With its Tuscan columns, vaulted ceilings, and ornate stucco work, the Isaac Synagogue remained an important religious fixture in Jewish Krakow until the outbreak of World War II. During the Nazi occupation of the city, the synagogue was looted, its chandeliers, tapestries, and religious objects stolen or destroyed. Soon after the Nazi attack on the building, the ransacked synagogue became a storehouse for theatrical props, and between 1943 and 1944 one of Krakow's most celebrated set designers used it as a workshop space.

A year after the war ended, the synagogue became a church and a cross was erected in the alcove that had once held the Ark. In the 1950s, with the Soviet secularization of the Polish state, the space was taken over by the Artists Unions of Krakow and was used as a workshop for sculptors. In the early 1970s the synagogue was converted for a brief time into a theater until the inside was badly damaged by fire. Left in disrepair, the damaged synagogue was taken over by the Historical Monuments Restoration workshop in 1983 when a renovation project was begun. Then, with the fall of the Soviet Union, the synagogue was returned to the Jewish community in 1989. Since that time, a number of renovation projects, financed by the city, have uncovered stucco work and Hebrew writings on the original stone walls. Since 1997, the partially restored synagogue serves as a prayer hall on Saturdays and a visitor and cultural center during other times of the week.[12]

As the history of the Isaac Synagogue reveals, Jewish spaces such as these stand as monuments to Jewish memory, illuminating a contentious Judeo-Christian history and the repeated de-sacrilization of Jewish spaces in Eastern Europe. Emerging out of this politicized cultural framework, the current usage of the synagogue as a museum and educational center illustrates how the movement to recover a "lost" Jewish heritage in Eastern Europe has chosen as its focus the pre-nineteenth-century world of Polish Hasidic life. To this end, the director of the Isaac Synagogue project explains:

> The majority of visitors who come here are simply trying to forge for themselves a picture of the past. ... People of various nationalities come here to deepen their knowledge of Jewish traditions and culture and discover more about the past of the Jewish people.[13]

In this search for the past, what visitors first encounter in the Isaac Synagogue are cardboard cut-outs of Hasidic men at prayer, two-dimensional figures that stand among the synagogue's wooden benches and against the original stone walls. The effect is not unlike walking into the Prague Synagogue during a Sabbath morning service. The memory there, as here, is one of men-only spaces, a return to a centuries-old Jewish world in which women were either absent or excluded. In this "world of our ancestors" mnemonic, the importance of women to the survival and to the persistence of the Jews as a religious people has been diminished. The Isaac Synagogue, as a Jewish monument, thus tells only part of the religious heritage of a vanquished society. In an effort to recall and re-imagine what had been lost to Poland, the installations of the Isaac Synagogue re-create an image and a vision of an isolated and distinctly male-centered Jewish world, a narrowly constructed portrayal that has become a defining lens through which Polish Jews are remembered and known. Such narrow constructions of Jewish religious culture appear frozen in time and religious space. As a trope of Polish culture, these memories position the Jew as the alien outsider whose pre-modern character remains in the forefront of national consciousness and whose difference and strangeness continue to inform an Eastern European construction of the Jewish interloper.[14] As my research at other heritage sites in Europe also revealed, this effect of Jewish memorialization is not unique to Poland and is found elsewhere in the European landscape, most notably in Germany's restored medieval tourist centers.

The pre-nineteenth-century German Jew and the reproduction of a gendered anti-Semitism

In keeping with Germany's commitment to the production of Jewish memory, the last two decades in this country have seen a growing interest in the restoration of its Jewish culture. Among the exhibits at the recently opened Jewish Museum in Berlin are installations that feature German Jewish life from the tenth to the nineteenth centuries. This set of exhibits begins with "The World of the Ashkenaz," an installation that highlights the importance of Worms, Speyer, and Mainz, the most significant Jewish communities of the Middle Ages. In the museum's celebration of Jewish medievalism, Germany appears to be engaged in a national project to secure a place for Germany's pre-modern Jews in the historical narratives of the nation's past. Prior to the Berlin museum's opening, the cities of Worms and Speyer had already begun to commemorate their medieval Jewish heritage with local and state initiatives that sought to excavate and restore medieval Jewish ruins within the city's borders. In the last decade, these places of Jewish memory have become major tourist sites, primarily for German tour groups which also visit the medieval churches of these historic cities. As places of Jewish heritage, the restored Jewish districts provide an interactive frame of remembrance through which the German visitor can inhabit vacant Jewish spaces that, historicized and lifeless, are unencumbered by the more problematic and difficult memories of a twentieth-century German Jewish history.

Among the most visited of these sites is the medieval quarter of Worms, whose renovation was sponsored by the city, with input from German scholars and in collaboration with a number of private

foundations. The historic district consists of two major thorough-
fares, the larger and smaller Judengasse (Jew's Street), and a complex
of restored buildings. Among the restorations are the rebuilt thirteenth-century men's and women's synagogues,[15] the Rashi Chapel, a
partially restored ritual bath, and the Rashi House Jewish museum.
The newly reconstructed synagogue, dedicated in 1961, incorporates
many modifications, including a modernized women's section. The
women's area of the synagogue incorporates part of the older synagogue and has since the 1980s served as a Holocaust memorial where
the names of the Jewish victims from Worms are commemorated
on the wall. Other references to the Holocaust include a plaque to a
woman teacher who tried to save the burning synagogue during the
1938 pogroms and a photograph of the re-consecration of the synagogue that dates to 1957. The two memorial plaques and the photograph are among the few references to a twentieth-century Jewish
community.

For the most part, the Jewish quarter in Worms focuses on
pre-nineteenth-century Jewish life and customs, tropes of a pre-
modern Jewish existence that are found both in the museum and
in the surviving ritual bath that was discovered just a few feet from
the synagogue ruins. The Rashi House museum, which is named
for the renowned eleventh-century scholar who studied briefly in
Worms, is built on the site of what is believed to be a former Jewish
dance hall. Designed to resemble a medieval community house of
the sixteenth century, the public areas of the museum consist of two
floors. The upper floor, through which visitors enter the museum,
contains an installation on the history of the Jewish community of
Worms, including stone fragments, charters, and maps that show
the partition of the city and the area where Jews were permitted to
reside. The lower floor, which is housed in a medieval stone cellar,
is presumed to be the original dance hall of the Jewish sector. It is
here where the pre-modern and medieval renderings of Jewish ritual
life have been re-created and placed on display. At the entry to the
lower-level exhibits, stand two life-size figures, a man and a woman
who represent the Jew and Jewess of medieval Worms. Based on
sixteenth-century illustrations by the artist Markus zum Lamm,

their dress reflects their Jewish status in German society. Each wears a cape bearing a yellow circular badge that, starting in 1584, was required of all Jews living in this region. The man, wearing a skull cap, carries a money bag and three bulbs of garlic (Figure 12). The text, as translated in the English-language museum catalog, describes the figures as follows:

> Two models show the *Customs of the Jews of Worms* around the year 1600. The man wears a black coat with yellow circular badge ("Judenfleck") and synagogue cap ("Schulkappe"). The woman is wearing a bonnet. The man is holding a money bag in his hand because he was a pawnbroker and a money changer. In the other hand he is carrying a bunch of garlic, consisting of three bulbs. In Hebrew, garlic is called *Shum* which is also the Hebrew abbreviation for the three large communities on the Rhine (Speyer, **W**orms, **M**ainz).[16]

Beyond these two life-size figures, a stairway leads to the main museum exhibitions that are housed in the medieval cellar. Although, as discussed in the previous chapter, these displays include a burned Torah from the Kristallnacht pogroms, the majority of the installations are thematically connected to pre-nineteenth-century Jewish life. Among the more unique of these exhibits is a set of dioramas that portray doll-size Jews in various scenes of eighteenth-century domesticity and ritual observance. In these exquisitely articulated installations, miniature Jewish families congregate around the Seder table, marry under a wedding canopy, and dine in a *sukkah* (an outdoor shelter) during the feast of the tabernacles. Created by a set designer especially for the museum, these imagined scenes of a peaceful and prosperous pre-nineteenth-century Jewish life suggest a fairytale-like existence in which wealthy Jewish patriarchs reign over their richly dressed wives and well-behaved children. In these renderings of Jewish family customs, elaborately decorated tables are laid with miniature silver candlesticks and coin-size pewter plates.

Sealed within a Plexiglas world, the Jewish miniatures appear safe and undisturbed. The narrative that accompanies the wedding

12. The Jew and Jewess of Worms.

diorama provides the only indication that a darker and more fearful version of pre-nineteenth-century Jewish life may have threatened the prosperity and peace of the Jewish middle class. In this text, the description of the diorama identifies the presence of an emissary of the local baron who was paid to protect the Jews from disturbances:

> An emissary of the Barons of Dalberg is present to prevent disturbances during the wedding (as well as during Jewish funerals). For this protection (*Judenshutz*) the Dalbergs (whose coat of arms is shown on the emissary's coat) are entitled to receive a fee.[17]

In this museum description, the use of the word "disturbances" is a guarded reference to the pogroms and anti-Jewish riots that began with the Crusades and persisted into the modern European era. Although the wedding scene alludes to the possibility of violence at Jewish ceremonies and gatherings, for the most part the idyllic domestic settings of the dioramas ignore this troubled history, creating in its stead an idealized memory of a tranquil and lavish lifestyle that, according to the museum's curator, is intended to show what is different and unique about the Jews and their religious customs.[18]

This construction of Jewish memory, while intended to highlight the beauty and depth of a family-based Jewish religious culture, nonetheless exoticizes the Jews who, having no modern German counterpart, appear as porcelain specimens preserved under glass. Even more problematic are the other tropes of memory that the life-size figures and the diorama installations suggest, promoting images of the Jews as prosperous and wealthy patriarchs contentedly celebrating rituals in well-appointed homes. Because there are no visual references to Jewish poverty or hardship, the scenes of ritual life convey a bourgeois opulence and elegance that reinforce the pervasive quality of Jewish wealth and thus the suspect nature of Jewish money lending and commerce. The classic diorama settings remind the visitor that Jews were not only outsiders in Christian Worms but that their money-lending ways served to increase their wealth and monetary success, perhaps to the detriment of their Christian neighbors.

Such a reading of the hand-crafted ritual installations is further complicated by another more pernicious memory that the Worms site conveys, a memory of the Jew that goes deeper into the German unconscious, beyond the motifs of Jewish wealth and greed, and into the more mythic and disturbing representations of the Jew as secretive, dangerous, and impure. These representations, associated primarily with the Middle Ages, are found in the museum's medieval drawings of Jewish practices and rituals that, set apart from the contrived setting of the diorama homes, create a darker and more ominous context for the memory of Jewish difference and religiosity. Two drawings in particular call to mind visual stereotypes that cast the Jews as deviant practitioners of a suspicious and perhaps demonic faith.

Jews and narratives of demonology

Showcased in a protective glass container, two book illustrations from the medieval period re-create the scene of a haunting and ominous Jewish cemetery whose unkempt and oddly shaped gravestones tumble over one another under a dark and cloud-filled sky. In this desolate and isolated landscape, two figures, a man and a child, stand alone before an eerily lit gravesite, the man's hand encircling the young child's shoulder. Solitary and bathed in an unnatural light, these figures do not appear to be mourners in any classical sense. Rather, the unusual and ominous surroundings of the cemetery invoke a feeling of suspicion, hinting at a more sinister memory of Jewish ritual and practice. Especially troubling is the presence of a young child in this death-filled landscape. Though the man, dressed in traditional Jewish religious attire, does not appear menacing or violent, the trope of ritual murder looms uneasily at the edges of this medieval rendering.

In the history of European anti-Semitism, the identification of Jews with the crime of ritual murder originates out of medieval mythologies that associate Jewish men with the devil, sorcery, magic, and the use of Christian blood, particularly that of a child, for the making of unleavened bread during Passover.[19] Such libels, while steeped in ancient folklore, persisted into the twentieth century and were embedded in the Nazi rhetoric of Jewish hatred. Nazi posters, now on display at the Dachau memorial, for example, show demonic figures rising out of haunted synagogues and lecherous and devil-like Jewish men ravishing innocent and terrified German women. Thus as Robert Wistrich explains:

> The Nazis exploited and secularized familiar medieval images of the Jew as Host desecrators, demons, sorcerers, well poisoners, and ritual murderers—as usurers, infidels, and insatiable conspirators seeking the destruction of Christian society. The Protestant Reformation in Germany and Martin Luther's mythologizing of the Jews as completely diabolical, provided an even more powerful arsenal of images for Nazi anti-Semitism.[20]

Medieval images, such as those in the Worms museum, that re-engage these tropes of Jewish demonology provide continuity for a repeated theme of anti-Semitism in which the Jews are represented as a force of evil and Satanic power.[21] In addition, such motifs also link Jewish men to pre-modern Christian witches (primarily women) who were also cast as sorcerers and devil worshippers. According to the historian Hugh Trevor-Roper, with the advent of the witch craze of the sixteenth and seventeenth centuries, Jews and witches became interchangeable categories of social and religious deviance, the men of one group and the women of the other each representing a force for evil and therefore a source of danger in Christian society.[22] The proliferation of theologies of demonology in which Jewish men and female witches were deemed as dangerous outsiders thus led to the development of a narrative in which female physiology was attributed to Jewish men, as Anne Barstow explains:

> The Germans thus had a dangerous heritage of violent persecution to use against any group perceived as deviant. Women as a gender suffered a special liability in that they had begun to be identified with the Jews. Both groups suffered from being associated with magical

practices: making potions and poisons. ... Rumors circulated about their bodies, that Jewish men menstruated (because they were circumcised), that witches bore the devil's mark, that both could turn themselves into animals. ... An especially damaging belief held against the Jews was that they celebrated a travesty of the Christian mass in which they worshipped the devil, requiring for communion either the bodies of Christians or their own sperm.[23]

Like other motifs of European Jewish memory, portraits of the medieval Jews as secretive ritual practitioners bring to mind anti-Semitic writings of later centuries that associate the body of Jewish men with that of women, each of which is marked by dangerous impurities.[24] As a subtext of Jewish memory, the notion of Jewish men's physical impurity and thus their feminine nature is further emphasized in the preservation of the *mikveh* (the Jewish ritual bath) as an important site of Jewish archaeology.

Gender, the Jewish ritual bath and German memory

While illustrations such as the medieval Jewish cemetery do not of themselves create a stigmatized memory of the pre-modern German Jew, their inclusion in this analysis is important because of the memorial setting in which these drawings are displayed. These illustrations, like the dioramas and the salvaged religious memorabilia of the Worms community, are enclosed in a subterranean museum space whose low and vaulted stone ceilings create a distinctly medieval environment. As such, the structural characteristics of the museum rooms foster a shift in time and place, as visitors descend into the medieval chambers that house a specifically time-bound Jewish memory. It is therefore not only the installations that link the Jews to a pre-modern identity but the buildings themselves that embed the Jew in a medieval archaeology, a special effect of commemoration that is made all the more convincing by the thirteenth-century ritual bath or *mikveh* that is also found at the Worms site.

According to the guide to Jewish historical places in Germany,

there are over 80 extant ritual baths in the country. These structures, which are found mostly underground, survived the destruction of synagogues over the preceding centuries of pogroms and
anti-Semitic violence. In an interesting manifestation of Holocaust
memory, many of the surviving mikvehs, such as the one previously
mentioned in Friedberg (Chapter 4), also serve as Holocaust memorials, bearing plaques to the lost Jewish citizenry of a town or city.
The ritual bath in Worms, which was donated to the community
in 1156 by Mordechai ben Joseph, is among the most architectur-
ally valuable Jewish monuments of its kind in Europe. Along with
the mikveh ruins in Cologne and Speyer, the elaborate stone bath
in Worms represents one of the most important remains of Jewish
mikvehs in the country. The ritual bath in Worms was first restored
in 1895 and then again in 1956, having been used as part of the
city's sewer system for at least a century. With the restorations, the
stonework of the mikveh has been repaired and the bath painstakingly
refurbished. Two stone tablets, bearing an original inscription, have
been placed in the mikveh's courtyard and tell of the donor's intent
and the mikveh's construction:

> The stone will cry and answer from the wall and the
> Scantling from its rafters
> He [Joseph] dug a well, erected the vault and cleared a path, a
> straight path, and the wall rests in its bay.

In keeping with the original design, large arched windows and
rounded niches are carved into the sides of the restored mikveh walls,
as a winding stairway, nearly 50ft below the ground, leads to a small
pool of water that is set in moss-covered medieval stones (Figure 13).
Like the entry into the medieval museum installation, a visit to the
Worms mikveh thus involves a descent into darkness. Reaching the
bottom of the steep stairway, the air becomes damp and the final
stairs of the bath are themselves underwater. Although the mikveh
waters, by religious law, must be derived from a natural spring, the
ritual bath here and elsewhere at archaeological sites in Germany
appears murky and polluted by the shiny coins and other objects that

13. The entry to the *mikveh*.

visitors have thrown into the small rectangular pool of water.

Situated far below the earth's surface, the *mikveh* is rife with visual allusions to hidden customs and secret passageways, taking the German sightseers into unseen places where the bodies of the Jews were purified in the dark recesses of the earth. As a place of Jewish memory, the *mikveh* invokes medieval references to Jews whose ritual lives took place in secret chambers, damp and unwelcoming spaces where they sought cleansing and purification. In language that refers to the *mikveh* as a "cave" and "a cultic center," the signage at the site explains the meaning of the *mikveh* in terms that recall the Jewish body as impure and the cave as a place of Jewish rites, tropes of medievalism that associate Jews with carnality and an underground Jewish hell that was popularized by medieval Christianity.[25]

What is perhaps most significant about the references to impurity is the absence of women as a category of remembrance. By the medieval period, ritual baths had mostly become associated with women's practices.[26] Although the original biblical concept of ritual impurity applied to both women and men, over time and by the medieval period the commandments of purification focused primarily on married women who were required to attend the *mikveh* after giving birth or at the end of their menstrual cycle, before resuming sexual relations with their husbands.[27] Judith Baskin, in her work on the Middle Ages, refers specifically to the *mikvehs* of Worms, Speyer, and Cologne, describing the central role that these ritual sites played in the lives of German Jewish women:

> Particular anxiety is expressed in several sources that women should not only be assiduous but also expeditious in observing these "family purity" regulations. Eleazar b. Samuel of Mainz advised his daughters to "scrupulously obey the rules applying to women:" They should carefully watch for the signs of their periods and keep separate from their husbands at such times. ... They shall be very punctilious and careful with their ritual bathing, taking with them women friends of worthy character.[28]

Despite the numerous historical references to the *mikveh* as essentially a women's space, none of the signage at Worms, Speyer, or Cologne distinguishes this ritual site as gendered.[29] The text which is mounted on the *mikveh* walls in Worms will help to illustrate this point:

> The *mikveh* is the ritual bath of the synagogue community. It was a square bath of living waters where the Jews came to purify themselves according to Leviticus Purity Laws. It was next to the synagogue of the medieval Jewish quarter and was topped by a tower that let light through.

In contrast to the traditional Jewish interpretation of the *mikveh*, in which women's bodies are typically singled out as polluting and dangerous to men, in the narratives of the German monuments, the Jewish male body becomes the frame through which Jewish purification and ritualized cleansing is recalled. Because all religious Jews of the medieval period are represented as men—the worshipper, the scholar, the ritualist, and the rabbi—it is particularly through men's bodies that the trope of impurity is given meaning in the *mikveh* narratives of Jewish custom and tradition. When these narratives are juxtaposed against the figure of Synagoga, whose image adorns the nearby Worms Cathedral (see Chapter 4), the effect of the *mikveh* site is compounded by the anti-Semitic motifs of the neighboring Christian iconography which feminizes the memory of Jewish law and Jewish patriarchy.

As these findings indicate, in the national-recovery projects that highlight the presence of the pre-modern European Jew, themes of impurity exist alongside motifs of wealth, family, and enlightenment, a memorial landscape that moves between images of the Jew as an elegant worshipper of an exotic faith and representations of the Jew as the foreign Other whose unknown and perhaps dangerous rituals took place in cemeteries and in underground caves. These two competing and frequently contradictory tropes of Jewish memory reveal the contradictions of German memorialization wherein the Jew is both exoticized and stigmatized. Writing on the image

of the Jew in German consciousness, Frank Stern described these
ambiguities as they first developed in a postwar German culture:

> Side by side with the concrete Jewish individual, another Jew
> existed in postwar German imagination, a kind of abstract Jew.
> The Jew that could be the accuser, the excessively wise sage
> (Lessing's *Nathan the Wise*), the "rich Jew," or the "wandering,
> homeless Jew," but also the "anti-German conspirator," or even the
> member of "certain circles" that were supposedly "too powerful,"
> "too influential." These idealized and stereotyped images of the
> Jews were at the center of the new postwar imagination.[30]

With the more recent shift toward the memorialization of pre-
modern German Jewry, these ambiguities have taken on new and
perhaps more harmful forms in which the "abstract and missing Jew"
has become both a source of a deep suspicion as well as a symbol of
national pride in the reclamation of Germany's pre-Holocaust past.

Engendering memory and the turn toward nostalgia in German and Eastern European representations of Jewish life and culture

In Pierre Nora's groundbreaking and voluminous work on the study
of memory, he discusses the relationship between a nation's obsession with collective memory and the shattering of national identity.[31] Citing the French obsession with memorial culture as an
example, he relates France's search for a "rediscovered heritage" to
"a deep consciousness of its threatened countryside, lost traditions,
wrecked ways of life—its very identity."[32] In Germany and Eastern
Europe, the trend toward the recovery of Jewish heritage speaks to
Nora's insights on collective memory as a means to restore a nation's
self-respect. As the findings of this chapter have demonstrated,
the commemoration of Jewish heritage within postwar European
cultures continues to be played out in two arenas. The first and most
obvious arena is that of Germany, whose national identity has yet to

recover from the rise of Nazism and the construction of the German nation as evil and genocidal.[33] The second arena, though less conspicuous and explicit, is the postwar tensions that have informed other European nations, such as Poland, whose complicity with the Nazi regime continues to be a source of contestation and unresolved self-blame. The celebration of pre-nineteenth-century Jewish memory in these countries can thus be understood as a national strategy for coping with the shattered identities of perpetrator nations. In re-inventing and valorizing pre-modern Jewish culture in diverse national settings, the memory of genocide and cultural annihilation is replaced with a nostalgic view of European Jewry that suggests tolerance and an appreciation for the Jewish Other in European memory.

The nostalgic turn in Holocaust memorialization has thus shaped national interest in Jewish religious culture throughout the German and Eastern European landscape.[34] In fostering medieval images of Jewish difference (and deviance), the tourist sites of Jewish history encourage the forgetting of modern genocide and facilitate the non-Jewish visitor's dis-identifcation from the twentieth-century victims of Nazi terror. Within the frame of religious memory more specifically, the valorization of Jewish medievalism obscures European Jewry's confrontations with modernity and, in so doing, ignores the rise of a more progressive form of Judaism in Poland and the establishment of reform Judaism in the more assimilated Jewish communities of Germany.[35] In comparison with twentieth-century representations of Jewish life and custom, the impressions that these sites create is one of a religious culture in which Jewish women are largely absent from the memoryscape of Jewish heritage, while Jewish men are both demonized and feminized by their representations in pre-modern religious culture.

This effect of nostalgia in Holocaust remembrance has thus created a trope of memory in which "All Jews are womanly, but no women are Jews."[36] The emergence of pre-nineteenth-century commemorative frameworks therefore compounds other forms of emasculating memory, such as those found in Kristallnacht memorialization, in which themes of victimization and humiliation figure prominently in Holocaust commemoration. In a complicated set of memorial representations, the interrelationship between the memory of the feminized Jewish male worshipper of earlier centuries and the emasculated Jewish male victim of the modern era come together to create a collective memory of the Jews that re-stigmatizes a people who can then be blamed for their own suffering and destruction.

Notes to Chapter 5

1. Pinto, Diana, "A new Jewish identity for post 1989 Europe," JPR Policy Paper, no.1 (1996), pp. 1–18.

2. *Ibid.*, p. 8.

3. Gruber, Ruth, *Virtually Jewish: Reinventing Jewish Culture in Europe* (Berkeley: University of California Press, 2002).

4. The origins of the synagogue's name are unknown, though there are two explanations. One derives from a myth that the stones of the synagogue were from the Second Temple and that they were brought to Prague by angels. According to this legend, after the Messiah arrives the stones must be returned to Jerusalem when a new temple will be built. The second story is that this synagogue replaced an older one and thus was the "new synagogue," but as other newer synagogues were built, this building, now the older structure, became the Old-New Synagogue.

5. In addition to this original women's section, a separate and more modern room was also available for women's seating, although this enclosed space did not allow a view of the sanctuary.

6. Vilnius in Lithuania has a similar but much less well-developed Jewish quarter where the rabbi and scholar Elijahu ben Shlomo Zalman ("the Goan of Vilna") lived and taught during the eighteenth century. Known as the "Jerusalem of Lithuania," Vilnius offers tours that include a visit to the Goan's prayer house, the place of his residence where a statue of the rabbi now stands, and the old Jewish market place.

7. Tyndall, Andrea, "Memory, authenticity and replication of the Shoah in museums," in Ronit, Lentin (ed), *Re-presenting the Shoah for the Twenty-first Century* (New York: Berghahn Books, 2004), pp. 112–94.

8. Fischer, Michael, "Working through the Other: The Jewish, Spanish, Turkish, Iranian, Ukrainian, Lithuanian, and German unconscious of Polish culture or one hand clapping: dialogue, silences and the mourning of Polish Romanticism," in G. Marcus (ed), *Perilous States* (Chicago: University of Chicago Press, 1993), pp. 224–8.

9. Gruber, *Virtually Jewish: Reinventing Jewish Culture in Europe.*

10. Gruber, *Virtually Jewish: Reinventing Jewish Culture in Europe*; Ray,

Larry, "Remembrance and ambiguity—sounds and spaces of klezmer 'revivals'," online paper, School of Social Policy and Social Research, University of Kent (Canterbury, UK, 2008), pp. 1–37.

11. Buber, Martin, *The Origin and Meaning of Hasidism* (New York: Horizon Press, 1960); Green, Alan, "Religion and mysticism; The case of Judaism," in J. Neusner (ed), *Take Judaism, for Example, Studies Toward the Comparison of Religions* (Chicago: University of Chicago Press, 1983).

12. Duda, Eugeniusz, *A Guide to Jewish Crakow* (Warsaw, 1990); Dybek, Dominik, "Isaac Synagogue,'" a tourist guide to the Isaac Synagogue project (Crakow, 2001).

13. Dybek, Dominik, "Isaac Synagogue," p. 5.

14. Fischer, "Working through the Other," in G. Marcus (ed), *Perilous States*, pp. 224–8.

15. In medieval Germany, Jewish communities such as Worms and Speyer built women's synagogues to accommodate women worshippers who were not permitted to pray in the sanctuary of the men's synagogue. This accommodation was seen as progressive as compared to synagogue designs, such as those in Prague, which seated women in walled-off spaces within the men's buildings.

16. Reuter, Fritz, *Jewish Worms: Rashi House and Judengasse*, trans Ursula Fritz (Worms: Heinrich Fischer, 1991).

17. *Ibid.*

18. *Ibid.*

19. Trachtenberg, Joshua, *The Devil and the Jews: The Medieval Conception of the Jew and Its Relation to Modern Anti-Semitism* (New Haven: Yale University Press, 1943); Wistrich, Robert, *Demonizing the Other: Anti-Semitism, Racism and Xenophobia* (The Netherlands: Harwood Academic Publishers, 1999).

20. Wistrich, *Demonizing the Other: Anti-Semitism, Racism and Xenophobia*, p. 3.

21. At Dachau the association of the Jew with the devil is portrayed in an exhibit on Nazi propaganda in which a lecherous Jewish man, with devil-like features, is shown ravishing a bound German woman. The caption reads: "Beware of the Jew."

22. Trevor-Roper, Hugh, *The European Witch-Craze of the Sixteenth and Seventeenth Centuries and Other Essays* (New York: Harper Collins, 1967).

23. Barstow, Anne Llewellyn, *Witchcraze: A New History of the European Witch Hunts* (New York: Pandora, 1995), p. 63.

24. Gilman, Sander, *Freud, Race and Gender* (Princeton: Princeton University Press, 1994).

25. Depictions of the Jewish hell in German Christian iconography include an underground cave where Jewish men are forced to sit on pigs while reading the Talmud, an image that is intended to show the Jew's perverse nature and absurd behavior. In this iconography, the figure of the devil shares the cave dwelling with the condemned Jews. See Schreckenberg, Heinz, *The Jews in Christian Art: An Illustrated History* (New York, Continuum, 1996), p. 250.

26. The laws regarding ritual purification are found in Leviticus and were originally intended to purify both men and women following the emission of bodily fluids. By the medieval period, the changing interpretations of Jewish law had recast the *mikveh* primarily as a woman's obligation and the baths mostly became women's ritual spaces. Men, especially during the high-holiday period, sometimes used the *mikveh* for ritual cleansing as well.

27. Wasserfall, Rahel (ed), *Women and Water: Menstruation in Jewish Life and Law* (Hanover, NH: Brandeis University Press, 1999); Biale, Rachel, *Women and Jewish Law: An Exploration of Women's Issues in Halakhic Sources* (New York: Schocken Books, 1984).

28. Baskin, Judith, "Jewish Women in the Middle Ages," in J. Baskin (ed), *Jewish Women in Historical Perspective* (Detroit: Wayne State University Press, 1998), p 116.

29. The one exception to this finding is in a small guide that was prepared by the German scholar Otto Boecher, and which is available at the museum bookstore. In the English version of this tourist guide, "The Old Synagogue in Worms on the Rhine," Boecher makes two important references to women and Jewish religious culture. The first refers to the *mikveh*: "The mikveh was used until the 18th century by members of the Jewish community in Worms for their ritual bath to re-gain ritual purity—in the end only women and very orthodox men." The second reference is to the women's synagogue: "Even though traditional Judaism exempted (and still exempts) women from participating in the religious cult, the Jews in the German Rhineland

particularly respected women and allowed them to participate indirectly in ceremonial life. Meir ben Joel and Judith, a childless couple like Jakob ben David and Rahel in 1034, donated a women's synagogue which adjoined the men's section in the north and was completed in 1212/13. The pointed arches which were opened up in 1842 and restored in 1959 between the men's and women's section represented a severe break with the old order; originally, the only links between the two buildings were a door and five small windows. A woman cantor would stand at the small windows and follow the service in the men's section and enable the women to join in the prayers. The first female cantor known by name was Urania, who died in 1275" (pp. 14–15).

30. Stern, Frank, "German-Jewish Relations in the Postwar Period: The Ambiguities of Anti-Semitic and Philosemitic Discourse," in Y.M. Bodemann (ed), *Jews, Germans, Memory: Reconstructions of Jewish Life in Germany* (Ann Harbor: University of Michigan Press, 1996), p. 94.

31. Nora, Pierre, (*Lieux de mémoire) Realms of Memory: Rethinking the French Past* (New York: Columbia University Press, 1996), pp. xv–xxiv.

32. *Ibid.*, p. xxii.

33. Giesen, Bernhard, "The trauma of perpetrators: The Holocaust as the Traumatic Reference of German national identity," in J. Alexander, R. Eyerman, B. Giesen, N. Smelser, and P. Sztompka (eds), *Cultural Trauma and Collective Memory* (Berkeley: University of California Press, 2004), pp. 112–54.

34. Typically, the study of nostalgia and mass trauma has been focused on the victims of mass violence rather than on the perpetrators. Thus the return to Hasidic forms of ultra-orthodoxy among contemporary Jewish groups, especially in Israel, has been in part explained as a response to the threat of annihilation and the desire to return to a way of life that marked the religiosity and simplicity of the pre-Holocaust Eastern European Jewish communities that today are being remembered and commemorated in Poland. As other scholars have noted, this trend within surviving traumatized societies frequently results in the return to traditional and rigid gender roles and the attending subordination of women in post-trauma societies. For a discussion of nostalgia as a victimized society's response to catastrophe, see Sztompka, Piotr,

"The trauma of social change: A case of post Communist societies," in J. Alexander, R. Eyerman, B. Giesen, N. Smelser, and P. Sztompka (eds), *Cultural Trauma and Collective Memory*, pp. 155–94; and Heilman, Samuel, *Defenders of the Faith: Inside Ultra-Orthdoxy* (New York: Schoken Books, 1992).

35. The Jewish reform or liberal movement had its origins in Germany in the nineteenth century and continued to develop as a progressive religious movement in Germany until the Holocaust. A significant aspect of this dimension of German Jewish history was the ordination of the first woman rabbi, Regina Jonas, by Rabbi Max Diebemann in Offenbach. In 1942 Rabbi Jonas was deported to Theresienstadt and then to Auschwitz where she died. There is a small exhibit to her memory at the Centrum Judaicum in the restored Neue Synagoge in Berlin.

36. Pellegrini, Ann, "Whiteface Performances: Race, gender, and Jewish bodies," in J. Boyarin and D. Boyarin (eds), *Jews and Other Differences: The New Jewish Cultural Studies* (Minneapolis: University of Minnesota Press, 1997), p. 109.

CHAPTER 6

RELATIONAL NARRATIVES IN SURVIVOR MEMORY AND THE FUTURE OF HOLOCAUST MEMORIALIZATION

Leaving the memorials and monuments of Eastern and Western Europe, the research in this concluding chapter offers a comparative framework through which to assess the construction of Holocaust memory from a gendered perspective. The focus for this comparative analysis are two Holocaust museums, one of which was founded by Holocaust survivors in Melbourne, Australia, and the other by a Holocaust survivor living in Terre Haute, Indiana. Although there are numerous Holocaust museums throughout North America and Australia, these two sites offer a unique perspective on collective memory and the role that first-generation survivors have assumed in creating "a space of one's own" in which to remember and commemorate the catastrophe of World War II. Fieldwork at both sites reveals a pattern of memorialization in which women's creativity and vision have been significant and where motifs of atrocity remembrance are contextualized by tropes of attachment and familial connection.

Family ties and atrocity narratives: the Holocaust Museum in Melbourne

The Holocaust Museum and Research Centre in Melbourne, Australia, was established in 1984 by a Holocaust survivor community whose members, having been denied entry into Palestine, settled in Melbourne in the postwar period. Nearly 40 years after their arrival in Australia, this group of survivors developed the Melbourne museum in response to the publicity surrounding David Irving and the Holocaust denial movement.[1] A founder of the museum thus described the museum's origins in the following way:

> Getting older, we become aware that our voices can't be heard forever. The [David] Irving interview was a turning point for me. I thought to myself, I am still alive and he tells me there was no Auschwitz. A lot of people reacted to that. A lot of survivors rang up the Holocaust Centre, wanting to deposit their memories, where before they couldn't talk about it.[2]

Housed in a former dance school, the museum was created through the efforts of the survivors who donated materials, art, artifacts, and photographs, as well as extensive monetary funds, to the museum project. The building sits on a small side street, tucked behind a section of the city where the postwar Jewish refugee population first made their home and later assimilated into Australian society. What is perhaps most distinctive about the museum site is the outdoor sculpture that, fixed to the outside walls of the museum, marks the space as a memory of Nazi atrocities and Jewish genocide. In a succession of bronze columns, the story of Jewish extermination unfolds in sculpted bronze plaques that document the arrest, deportation, and murder of European Jews. Framed by disembodied hands reaching out for help, Hebrew letters that represent the word for life, and twisted knots of barbed-wire fencing, the bronzed images are reproductions of atrocity photographs. These small sculptures, each connected to one another, show naked women and children running to the gas chambers, skeletal corpses lying in open pits, and men and women about to be massacred. Cast in bronze, these figurative scenes occupy a public area that borders a small but open urban thoroughfare, bringing into sharp relief the terrible and frightening history of World War II.

Once inside the museum building, the memorial space takes on multiple levels of meaning and expression. Since its initial development, the museum has been remodeled and expanded to include an exhibition space, a library, and a room for educational programs. The galleries in the museum are organized around seven themes: The Vanished World, Rise of Nazism, Ghetto Life, Mass Executions, The Camp System, Resistance to the Holocaust, and Children. The first installation that the visitor encounters is that of The Vanished World, a display of family photographs that were compiled by the founders of the museum, many of whom are women and who currently serve as museum guides. The text that introduces the first installation situates the museum within survivor culture and conveys the importance of relationality as a motif of remembrance:

Our Guides' Families

The guides are the backbone of this museum. Most of them are survivors of the Holocaust or descendants of survivors. These photos of their families were taken in peaceful times before their world was overturned by the Holocaust. Wedding photos, family portraits, children at play—these are glimpses into the past lives of our guides' families. This is the world that vanished when Hitler came to power and began implementing his plans for the destruction of European Jewry.

The exhibit of family portraits includes a vast array of images. Actors from the Yiddish theater appear alongside Jewish intellectuals and athletes. Multi-generational photographs show extended families with children at play, at school, and in studio-style portraiture. Captions identify the persons in the photographs in relation to the museum's founders and to the guides who welcome the visitor into the memorial space. In one photograph, a couple is shown leaning in toward one another, serious and yet intimate in front of the camera. The caption reads:

Zosia & Julek Siegreich (parents of guide Ruth Crane). Taken from Ghetto Bedzin to Auschwitz; perished in 1943. Photo taken 1926 in Siemanowice.

Another picture, clearly a studio portrait, shows a young girl facing the camera, pen and paper at her side, a faint smile on her face. The texts below this poignant image reads:

> Stanislawa Pohl (aunt of guide Halina Zylberman). Living on false papers, was betrayed in her thirties, died in Warsaw in 1942.

Together with the texts, the photographs in The Vanished World exhibit document the loss of family members and the survivor's relationship to those who died. Within this relational paradigm it is possible to view the Our Guides' Families installation as an expression of women's culture, commemorating the place that relationships assume in the remembrance of trauma and loss. Accordingly, the work of the self-in-relation theorists provides a useful perspective through which to consider this form of family-based memorialization.[3] In particular, Carol Gilligan's research on women and development helps to contextualize the importance of connection and attachment in the Melbourne exhibit:

> The psychology of women that has consistently been described as distinctive in its greater orientation toward relationships and interdependence implies a more contextual mode of judgment and a different moral understanding. Given the differences in women's conception of self and morality, women bring to the life cycle a different point of view and order human experience in terms of different priorities. ... The elusive mystery of women's development lies in its recognition of the continuing importance of attachment in the human life cycle.[4]

As Gilligan's theory suggests, the tropes of family ties and attachments that preside over the images in The Vanished World gallery allow for an ongoing relationship with those who have died, making possible a continued connection to a mother, aunt, or cousin whose death and suffering is framed by a "living" memory of prewar life. Such framing, which in part has been created by women survivors, becomes especially significant when juxtaposed against the other installations that make up the remainder of the museum space.

Just past the family gallery exhibit, the museum opens up into an interior space where the terror of the Holocaust is commemorated and re-lived in photographs and art work that, like the memorial at Auschwitz, re-creates in graphic imagery the memory of atrocities. Although portraits and sculptures of mothers and children are also found within this exhibition hall, the predominant motifs are clearly those of incarceration and death. The centerpiece of this area is an intricate and carefully executed model of Treblinka that was designed and built by Chaim Sztajer, a survivor who spent three years re-creating the concentration camp where he had been incarcerated and where his family perished.[5] Other art work, particularly by the sculptor and guide Sarah Saaroni, show women prisoners in despair. Saaroni's poignant and moving representations feature starved and frail inmates living in the camp barracks and holding one another in their arms. These three-dimensional pieces, which are interspersed throughout the museum, are surrounded by photographs that have been collected from a diverse and varied set of archives which document the mass executions in Latvia, Germany, and Poland, as well as the systematic starvation of women prisoners.

Among these numerous atrocity photographs, a group of pictures, similar to those at Auschwitz, display the bodies of starved Jewish women at liberation. Among these, one image in particular stands out as a more candid, less posed, and therefore less protective memory of the subject. In this photograph, a naked woman is shown walking between two hospital beds. Unable to stand alone, her arms grasp the beds' metal posts for support. In this image, the woman's entire body is visible to the camera (and thus to the viewer in the museum), her breasts and genitals uncovered and revealed.

A second photograph in a nearby collection of execution scenes similarly exposes the unprotected and exposed bodies of Jewish men and boys. Taken in Poland by the resistance movement, this picture is a well-known and well-disseminated photograph of Jewish prisoners standing before an open pit in a secluded forest.[6] As an especially telling study of gendered memory, this photograph represents a confluence of Holocaust motifs that bring together the images of naked and powerless Jewish men with their Nazi executioners. The brief accompanying text offers only this observation: "naked Jews humiliated before execution." This narrative clearly articulates the relationship between Jewish men's humiliation and captivity, conveying a sense of shame for the Jewish prisoners whose nakedness symbolizes both their imminent death and their emasculation by the Nazi perpetrators.

The use of this atrocity image, as well as those of starvation and torture, reveals the extent to which survivor memory, 40 years after the war, sought to memorialize and recall the most heinous of Nazi crimes while, at the same time, contextualizing these memories within relationship motifs that humanized the representations of the Nazi victim. This tension between representations of familial connections and the remembrance of atrocity and violence appears to be characteristic of survivor memory, revealing the complex ways in which collective memorialization is informed both by women's experience of connectivity in trauma and a longing, among both women and men, to authentically and unsparingly commemorate the horrors of the past. Within this framework of remembrance, a mnemonic of atrocity accompanies the tropes of relationship, creating a narrative of mass violence where connections to individual victims become possible. This narrative of memorialization, in which atrocity memory and relationship motifs are set against one another, is typical of other survivor-inspired installations and is also found at the CANDLES Museum in Terra Haute, Indiana.

The CANDLES Museum: memorializing family and the memory of Auschwitz

Located in a city that has suffered the effects of a declining economy, the CANDLES Museum and Education Center is an anomaly among the numerous and well-funded Holocaust museums and memorials throughout the United States. Housed in a single-story brick building, the museum sits amidst strip malls and fast-food restaurants that have come to define so much of Mid Western urban life. In keeping with the billboard advertising that surrounds the museum, the sign for CANDLES is nearly 20ft tall and, with bold lettering, proclaims the mission of the center: "Let us remove all hatred and prejudice from our world. Let it begin with Me," and "Holocaust Education Promotes Peace." Amidst the advertisements for car repairs and fast-food restaurants, the CANDLES' large and prominent sign is thus a call for tolerance and awareness in a most unlikely commercial landscape.

Founded by Eva Kor, a child survivor of Mengele's twin experiments, the name of the center derives from an acronym for C(hildren) of A(uschwitz) N(azi) D(eadly) L(ab) E(experiments), a group that Kor started in 1984 and whose name later became the designation by which the museum is now known. Since the museum's opening in 1995, Kor has remained the central figure of this memorial space, creating and maintaining the exhibits, lecturing in outreach programs, and overseeing the center's educational programs. Within the larger sphere of US memorial culture, however, Kor is considered somewhat of an "outsider" whose stance on forgiveness has been a source of tension within the survivor community. Since the making of the documentary film *Forgiving Mengele* (2006), in which Kor is featured, she (as well as the museum) has been at the center of an ongoing controversy on the appropriateness of forgiving Nazi perpetrators.[7] Despite the controversy that surrounds her, the act of forgiving remains a fundamental value for Kor. The website of the museum thus includes her ideas on forgiveness as a means to recovery and healing:

> I believe with every fiber of my being that every person has the human right to live with or without the pain of the past, and that it is a personal choice. My question is, "How many people would choose to live with pain, when they could heal from it?"
>
> I do believe that this healing is possible through the act of FORGIVENESS and I believe in FORGIVENESS as the ultimate act of self healing, and self empowerment. Once a person decides to forgive, there is a tremendous feeling of wholeness in thought, spirit and action all moving in the same direction creating a

powerful force for healing and freedom.

My forgiving the Nazis is a gift of freedom I gave myself, a gift of peace for myself, it is also a gift of peace for everybody who wants it. Both peace and war begin in the heart and mind of one person. Pain and anger are the SEEDS for WAR. FORGIVENESS is the SEED for PEACE!

During my two-day visit to the museum, I had the opportunity to interview Kor, to record and photograph the museum exhibits, and to observe Kor as she guided visitors through the installations, recounting her family history and her commitment to forgiveness as source of empowerment for Nazi victims. From the moment one enters the museum space, the imprint of Kor's vision and memory frames this site of remembrance. From the museum lobby, where shoes for a Darfur project fill the entry way, to the display cases that are lined with taffeta from Kor's dresses, each space represents this survivor's unique and personal vision of memorial culture. The museum that Kor designed includes thematic exhibits that show-case artifacts, photographs, posters, and newspaper clippings, some of which were donated and others of which she purchased for the museum. These displays give an account of the rise of Nazism, the history of the medical experiments, the experiences of her family, and Kor's postwar reconciliation with the German perpetra-tors. Although these various installations give an overall account of Nazism and especially of the twin experiments, the motifs that arouse the deepest feelings and an emotional connection to the past are those that highlight family loss and the deep bonds of sisterhood that informed Kor's vision of the museum's mission and its themes of remembrance.

In many ways, the narratives of the museum express the deep and life-long attachment between two sisters, each of whom occupies a central role in the remembrance of the Holocaust through the history of the twin experiments. Eva and her sister Miriam were deported, along with their parents and older siblings, from Hungary (Transyl-vania) to Auschwitz. While the rest of the family died at Auschwitz, the ten-year-old twin sisters, selected for experimentation, survived, although each suffered life-long medical problems from exposure to bacteria and disease. Although Kor had considered establishing a museum for many years, it was not until her sister's death in 1993 from cancer that her goals for the museum were realized, as she explains:

> I was devastated when she died. I was left with a lot of pain and I developed nightmares. I could feel how Miriam died, how the cancer came into her lungs and she couldn't breathe. I knew all along that some day I wanted a museum. I was trying to figure out what I could do in her memory, what I could do to remove part of my pain because I knew if I did something in her memory that it would remove the focus from "me, poor me" and what happened to me and use it for something good.

In keeping with her dedication to her sister, the exhibition space at CANDLES begins with a set of family photographs that feature Eva, Miriam, their parents, and their sisters. The family installation shows Eva and Miriam at age one and then again as young children, posing for the last time with their parents and siblings in a garden-like setting. The text that accompanies this photograph is a narrative of personal loss:

> As I walked from room to room to try to find any reminder, any remnants of the life we once lived, I found one badly crumpled picture. This the last picture of the family. It was taken in late Fall 1943. My sister Miriam and I are sitting alongside our mother. ... Today I am the only family member surviving.

On the opposite wall from this visual and public remembrance, a photograph of children being liberated from Auschwitz shows the ten-year-old Eva and Miriam, dressed in striped overcoats and woolen hats, leading the line of other children out of the camp barracks. The date is January 27, 1945. Nearly five decades later, the sisters return to Auschwitz and are photographed in matching blue coats, scarves, and red hats as they stand on the snow-covered grounds of the camp memorial, pictured at the same barracks from which they had been liberated 50 years earlier. The juxtaposition of the two images is powerful and moving, conveying the interconnectedness between two women whose sisterhood and shared past converge in a memory of atrocity and survival. Two years after the 1991 trip to Auschwitz, Miriam died and in a final tribute to her sister, Kor installed a memorial to Miriam in the museum's library. Among the artifacts and documents in this display is a framed sweat shirt bearing two images: the picture of the young twins during the 1945 liberation and a photograph of the sisters' return to Auschwitz in 1991. The words, "I miss you Miriam," are printed across the bottom of the shirt.

In addition to the photographs of Miriam and Eva, the exhibit on the Auschwitz twins recounts the history of Mengele's experiments. This documentation includes pictures of the children being examined and measured by the Nazi medical workers, pictures of starved and naked children, and prewar and postwar photographs of numerous pairs of twins who survived the war. Thus the very nature of the museum's mission, to remember and honor the suffering and experiences of the children who were subject to the twin experiments, brings into focus the memory of siblings whose biological connection to one another determined their fate at Auschwitz and in many cases led to their survival. The memory of the twin experiments therefore offers a complicated set of tropes: the atrocity of experimentation, crimes specifically against Jewish children, and the bonds of love and kinship between siblings whose abuse at Auschwitz and whose survival frames the tragedy of the Holocaust through narratives of family images that bring a personal dimension to the construction of collective memory.

Taken together, the familial tropes of memory that define the memorial spaces of both the CANDLES exhibits and the installations of the Melbourne museum have helped to re-define and re-conceptualize alternative approaches to the remembrance of genocide. In these unique places of memory, first-generation/survivors have constructed their own memorial culture, establishing museums and monuments that bring to the memorial site a survivor's sensibility and a desire to represent the past as they wish it to be remembered—through their relationship and attachment to family, friends, and children. It is significant to point out that a similar frame of memory, inspired by another woman survivor, has also been incorporated into the Holocaust Memorial Museum in Washington, DC. The renowned Tower of Faces installation features photographs from the prewar life of the Jews from Ejszyski, a Lithuanian *shtetl* (village). The photographs in this collection were donated by Yaffa Eliach who, like Eva Kor, was a child survivor. Having salvaged the life work of her grandparents, themselves professional photographers, Eliach offered to donate hundreds of images of Jewish families, friends, team mates, and workers to the museum's permanent collection.[8]

After some initial reluctance on the part of the planning committee, the museum eventually agreed to house the exhibit and to build a special exhibition space, creating what, in retrospect, has become one of the most lauded and evocative displays in the entire collection. In a multi-level tower-shaped gallery, the family portraits and photographs of domesticity humanize the face of Jewish victimhood through representations of a diverse Jewish community that was culturally and socially engaged with the world around it. As Marianne Hirsch explains, the connective function of this installation is grounded in the familial context through which these particular Jewish citizens are recalled:

> We might leaf through any of our family albums and find similar photos. But if the tower is a family album, then we are situated right inside it. Like all family albums, the tower preserves and creates memory: it is a site of remembrance and commemoration. ... When we enter the Tower of Faces, we leave the historical account of the museum and enter a domestic space of a family album that shapes a different form of looking and knowing, a different style of recognition, one that is available to any viewer and that can connect viewers of different backgrounds to one another.[9]

In part, the ability of the Tower exhibit to transcend the Jewish experience and to foster a cross-cultural identification among viewers lies in this exhibit's relation-based narrative, as the motifs of family and kinship universalize the extent to which loss and human tragedy is central to the commemoration of the Holocaust. Like the family-centered exhibits in the Melbourne and CANDLES museums, the Lithuanian installation was born out of a survivor's vision of remembrance that, with its focus on family, domesticity, and relationship, has transformed the culture of Holocaust memorialization through visual representations that connect the viewer to the living culture of the prewar Jews and to the meaning of personal loss within a larger narrative of mass trauma.

Concluding thoughts: gendered memory and the future of Holocaust memorialization

The research I conducted at the CANDLES museum was the last site of memory that I studied for this project. In leaving Indiana, I was struck by the places where the project had taken me, from the monuments at Auschwitz and Majdanek to the memorial centers of Melbourne and Terra Haute. In between these sites, there had been over 100 other fieldwork settings where the remembrance of genocide and violence had left their mark and where multiple frames of collective memory have been preserved, created, and re-created over more than half a century of post-Holocaust memorialization. As I left Terra Haute I found my thoughts returning to the places of memory where the project first began—the concentration and death-camp memorials of Eastern Europe—spaces of commemoration where images of horror and dehumanization prevail. As my thoughts returned to these atrocity-filled landscapes, I was reminded of an important essay by the historian Claudia Koontz, whose writings suggest that such topographies of evil must be preserved as "warnings" for the future:

> Standing as monuments to unspeakable crimes, these camps command their visitors to ponder the depths of evil, "Pause. Stop. And think," they seem to say. Indeed, the German word

for monument, *Denkmal*, conveys that meaning. For concentration camp sites, a new noun, *Mahnmal*, commands us to take warning. At these places of remembering (*Gedenkstaette*), memory feels monolithic, unambiguous, and terrible. A violent past haunts the present there. ... The enduring legacy of the camps, however, must be to serve as warnings (*Maehnmaler*) against all forms of political terror and racial hatred.[10]

In reviewing the research that I have presented here and my own observations at these sites of terror, I remain conflicted about the role that atrocity memory has come to play in the remembrance of the Holocaust. On the one hand, I agree with Koontz—these monuments must stand as reminders of the human capacity for violence and hatred. Having visited so many of these places of death and suffering, I fully appreciate the national, local, and foundational efforts that have gone into the preservation of these camps and I am grateful for the work that has been done to more accurately represent this terrible period of European history. At the same time, I remain troubled by the unintended consequences of memorialization. As the discussions of the previous chapters have shown, the camps, as well as other sites of Jewish memory, form a complicated culture of collective memory in which issues of gender, anti-Semitism, and representations of victimization have yet to be resolved.

Beginning with the analyses of Auschwitz and Ravensbrück, it is clear that memorializing women in monuments to genocide poses challenges both for the perpetrator nations and the victimized populations who seek to tell the tragic truths of persecution while honoring the memory of those who were violated and murdered. At Auschwitz, it is the repetitive tropes of the embodied woman prisoner that convey the horror and dehumanization of the Holocaust subject. These images, although riveting, leave the formerly imprisoned woman unprotected and therefore vulnerable to the visitor's gaze. Because of the thousands of people who pass through these halls and exhibits every year, it is impossible to gauge the effect on public consciousness. Do the citizens of the perpetrator nations see a "Jewish" body ravished by deprivation and torture, or do they see the female body, stripped bare and naked, forever frozen in time in the halls of the concentration camp? Do women visitors see themselves reflected in the representations of violation and despair and do the men who tour the memorial see an "object of "desire whose image of powerlessness is permanently fixed in visual narratives of terror and subjugation? And what of the Jews who make pilgrimages to the death-camp sites, what do they see? Do they witness the helplessness of Jewish mothers and grandmothers whose suffering has become the domain of public memory, or do they see a Jewish people, humiliated, decimated, and destroyed?

At Ravensbrück, where Jewish tour groups rarely go, the gaze is mostly that of German tourists and schoolchildren whose perspective on the Nazi past is framed by international images that situate the memory of genocide in a universal narrative of gendered violence. And what is remembered here? The sadism of the women guards— the fear always of women's rage turning against other women? The loneliness of suffering and the will to survive in a wasteland of death? Do the visitors, especially the schoolchildren, leave with a memory of maternal sacrifice that is the inevitable fate of mothers who are powerless to prevent war, or do they fixate on the prison cells, the torture rooms, and the more sensationalized narratives of a women's prison where whips and death carts mark the memoryscape of the monument? And finally, do the international tropes of women's victimization at Ravensbrück encourage a "non-Jewish" reading of the Nazi regime—a more universalizing memory in which the Jews become only a small and somewhat insignificant part of a national memory of shame and guilt?

These and other questions are further complicated by the "other" gendered reading of Jewish genocide—the one in which representations of numerous, diverse, and repeated tropes of victimization call into question the masculinity of Jewish men and the viability of a Jewish patriarchy to confront and challenge the Nazi aggressors. In the work that has been presented here, the research pushes the boundaries of a gendered analysis beyond the images of passive male prisoners and unprotected women and children and into the realm of other symbolic systems, most notably those that represent the desecrated and violated synagogue. It is here where the less obvious and perhaps more detrimental effects of Holocaust memory seep into public consciousness in unanticipated ways. As institutional Judaism is symbolized by a patriarchal tradition that is defined by the power of a patriarchal God, the "failure" of this God has been commemorated in visual narratives of Kristallnacht pogroms in which the synagogue and the Torah become stand-ins not only for the slaughtered Jewish people but for a Jewish God whose violation has informed both the public memory of German history and the Jewish memory of sorrow and loss.

The emasculating tropes of the violation of the Jewish sacred are linked to other motifs of memory that feminize the Jewish male. At sites of medieval Jewish culture, the conflation of Jewish men's impurity with that of women adds yet another lens through which the Jew is "Othered" and vilified in narratives of religious practice and ritual observance that re-inscribe into European consciousness medieval fears of Jewish evil and the "darker elements" of the Jewish temperament. Without a modern visual world in which to contrast these and other images of pre-nineteenth-century Jews, remembrance can become a dangerous obsession that regenerates and revitalizes anti-Semitic stereotypes that have never totally disappeared from European culture and that continue to inform both the memory of the perpetrator nations and the post-genocide consciousness of the victimized populations.

As images of a humiliated, passive, and demonized Jewish people have become embedded in the Holocaust narrative, themes of victim blaming and Jewish shame have become intertwined with the discourse on memorialization. Research on Eastern European responses to the Holocaust reveal a troubling pattern of historical revisionism in which the passive and non-resistant Jew has been held accountable for the annihilation of the Jewish people.[11] Simultaneously, Jewish self-blame and shame for the Holocaust remains an unspoken but pervasive subtext of Jewish memory. To "never forget" the genocide of the Nazi regime is to remember always the powerlessness of Jewish men. In this regard, Israeli feminist scholars such as Ronit Lentin have interrogated the impact of the memory of Jewish emasculation on Israeli militarism and nationalism. In a compelling analysis of the founding of the state of Israel, Lentin describes a split in the developing consciousness of the young Jewish state, as the early settlers were cast as strong and powerfully aggressive pioneers while Holocaust refugees were viewed as weak and passive "remnants" of a humiliated European Jewry.[12] In the decades since the founding of the state, Lentin and other feminist scholars have argued that the association of the Holocaust with a weak and emasculated Jewish people remains a significant mnemonic of Israeli Holocaust remembrance.[13] With the continued development and expansion of Holocaust memorials worldwide, the image of the feminized and humiliated Jewish male is inescapable. To compensate and cope with this postwar memory, notions of a Jewish hyper-masculinity have been idealized and reified both in Israel and in the wider transnational Jewish community that has constructed the Holocaust as a marker of a victimized Jewish identity.

Given these and other consequences of Holocaust memorialization, the question then becomes, what are the alternatives? How do societies recall the truth of a violent past without humiliating and shaming the subjects of oppression? The motifs and tropes of the survivor-inspired memorials and museums suggest one important answer to these questions. In particular, the focus on the relational world of the victims and the survivors can bring a more nuanced and humanity-driven perspective to the recollections of subjugation and horror. In looking toward the future, the inclusion of narratives of relationship and connectivity can provide an alternative to the voyeuristic, emasculating, and numbing effects of so many of the existing representations. In searching out the means by which the memories of mass trauma and violence are preserved and recorded, a balance must be struck between the documentation of terror and the representation of humanity in the aftermath of genocide. While the former may act as a warning for future generations, such a warning will have little efficacy if the frames of commemoration dehumanize the subject and denigrate the memory of those who can no longer speak for or represent themselves.

Notes to Chapter 6

1. Berman, Judith, "Australian representations of the Holocaust: Jewish Holocaust museums in Melbourne, Perth, and Sydney, 1984–1996," *Holocaust and Genocide Studies* 13 (1999), pp. 200–1.

2. *Ibid.*, p. 202.

3. Chodorow, Nancy, *The Reproduction of Mothering: Psychoanalysis and the Sociology of Gender* (Berkeley: University of California Press, 1978); Gilligan, Carol, *In a Different Voice: Psychological Theory and Women's Development* (Cambridge, MA: Harvard University Press, 1982); Jordan, Judith, Alexandra Kaplan, Jean Baker Miller, Irene Stiver, and Janet Surry, *Women's Growth In Connection: Writings from the Stone Center* (New York: Guilford Press, 1991).

4. Gilligan, *In a Different Voice: Psychological Theory and Women's Development*, pp. 22–3.

5. Chaim Sztajer was one of about 100 Jewish survivors of Treblinka. He died in 2008 at the age of 98.

6. Among other memorials, this photograph is found in the Jewish Pavilion at Auschwitz and in the Wanasee museum and memorial outside Berlin. It is also the opening image for Janina Struk's book *Photographing the Holocaust* (London: I.B.Tauris, 2004).

7. Because of the objections of other Holocaust survivors, a screening of the film was canceled by the United Nations during the 2009 commemoration of Holocaust Remembrance week.

8. Hirsch, Marianne, *Family Frames: Photography, Narrative and Postmemory* (Cambridge, MA: Harvard University Press, 1997); Leninthal, Edward, *Preserving Memory: The Struggle to Create America's Holocaust Museum* (New York: Viking, 1995).

9. Hirsch, *Family Frames: Photography, Narrative and Postmemory*, pp. 252–4.

10. Koontz, Claudia, "Between memory and oblivion: Concentration camps in German memory," in J. Gillis (ed), *Commemorations: The Politics of National Identity* (Princeton, NJ: Princeton University Press, 1994), pp. 259, 275.

11. Mushkat, Marian, *Philo-semitic and Anti-Jewish Attitudes in Post Holocaust Poland* (Lewiston, NY: Edwin Mellen Press, 1992); Irwin-Zarecka,

Iwona, *Frames of Remembrance: The Dynamics of Collective Memory* (New Brunswick, NJ: Transaction Publishers, 1994).

12. Lentin, Ronit, *Israel and the Daughters of the Shoah: Reoccupying the Territories of Silence* (New York: Berghahn Books, 2000).

13. Sered, Susan, *What Makes Women Sick? Maternity, Modesty and Militarism in Israeli Society* (Hanover, NH: Brandeis University Press, 2000).

BIBLIOGRAPHY

Alexander, Jeffrey, "On the social construction of moral universes: The Holocaust from war crime to trauma drama," in J. Alexander, R. Eyerman, B. Giesen, N. Smelser, and P. Sztompka (eds), *Cultural Trauma and Collective Memory* (Berkeley: University of California Press, 2004)

Azaryahu, Maoz, "RePlacing memory: The reorientation of Buchenwald," *Cultural Geographies* 10 (2003), pp. 1–20

Baer, Ulrich, "To give memory a place: Holocaust photography and landscape tradition," *Representations* 69 (2000), pp. 38–62

Barstow, Anne Llewellyn, *Witchcraze: A New History of the European Witch Hunts* (New York: Pandora, 1995)

Baskin, Judith, "Jewish Women in the Middle Ages," in J. Baskin (ed), *Jewish Women in Historical Perspective* (Detroit: Wayne State University Press, 1998)

Baumel, Judith Tydor, *Double Jeopardy: Gender and the Holocaust* (London: Valentine Mitchell, 1998)

____, "Women's agency and survival strategies during the Holocaust," *Women's International Forum* 22 (1999), pp. 329–47

Becker, Howard (ed), *Exploring Society Photographically* (Evanston, Ill: Northwestern University Press, 1981)

Behar, Ruth, "Writing in my father's name: A diary of *Translated Woman's* first year," in R. Behar and D.A. Gordon (eds), *Women Writing Culture* (Berkeley: University of California Press, 1995)

Berman, Judith, "Australian representations of the Holocaust: Jewish Holocaust museums in Melbourne, Perth, and Sydney, 1984–1996," *Holocaust and Genocide Studies* 13 (1999), pp. 200–21

Biale, Rachel, *Women and Jewish Law: An Exploration of Women's Issues in Halakhic Sources* (New York: Schocken Books, 1984)

Bodemann, Y. Michal (ed), *Jews, Germans, Memory: Reconstuctions of Jewish Life in Germany* (Ann Arbor, MI: University of Michigan Press, 1996)

——, "Reconstructions of history: From Jewish memory to nationalized commemoration of Kristallnacht in Germany," in Bodemann, Y. Michal (ed), *Jews, Germans, Memory: Reconstructions of Jewish Life in Germany* (Ann Arbor, MI: University of Michigan Press, 1996)

Bondy, Ruth, "Women in Theresienstadt and the family camp in Birkenau," in D. Ofer and L. Weitzman (eds), *Women and the Holocaust* (New Haven: Yale University Press, 1998)

Boose, Lynda, "Crossing the River Drina: Bosnian rape camps, Turkish impalement, and Serb cultural memory," *Signs: A Journal of Women, Culture and Society* 28 (2002), pp. 20–38

Buber, Martin, *The Origin and Meaning of Hasidism* (New York: Horizon Press, 1960)

Carrier, Peter, *Holocaust Monuments and National Memory Cultures in France and Germany since 1989* (New York: Berghahn Books, 2005)

Chapman, Elizabeth, *Sociology and Visual Representations* (New York: Routledge, 1994)

Chodorow, Nancy, *The Reproduction of Mothering: Psychoanalysis and the Sociology of Gender* (Berkeley: University of California Press, 1978)

Connerton, Paul, *How Societies Remember* (London: Cambridge University Press, 1989)

Davidman, Lynn, "Truth, subjectivity and ethnographic research," in J. Spikard and S. Landres (eds), *Personal Knowledge and Beyond* (New York: New York University Press, 2002)

DeSilva, Cara, *In Memory's Kitchen: A Legacy from the Women of Terezin* (New Jersey: Jason Aronson, 1996)

DeVault, Marjorie, *Liberating Method: Feminism and Social Research* (Philadelphia: Temple University Press, 1998)

Domansky, Elisabeth, "Kristallnacht, the Holocaust and German unity: The meaning of November 9 as an anniversary in Germany," *History and Memory* 4 (1992), pp. 60–93

Duda, Eugeniuszu, *A Guide to Jewish Cracow* (Warsaw, 1990)

Durkheim, Émile, *The Elementary Forms of Religious Life* (Oxford: Oxford University Press, 2001)

Eimer, Colin, "Jewish and Christian suffering," in D. Cohn-Sherbok (ed), *Holocaust Theology: A Reader* (New York: New York University Press, 2002)

Eschebach, Insa, "Engendered oblivion: Commemorating Jewish inmates at the Ravensbrück Memorial," in J.T. Baumel and T. Cohen (eds), *Gender, Place and Memory in the Modern Jewish Experience* (London: Valentine Mitchell, 2003)

Fausto-Sterling, Anne, "Gender, race, and nation: The contemporary anatomy of 'Hottentot' women in Europe, 1815–1817," in J. Terry and J. Urla (eds), *Deviant Bodies* (Bloomington: Indiana University Press, 1995)

Feinstien, Margarete, "Absent fathers, present mothers: Images of parenthood in Holocaust survivor narratives," *Nashim: A Journal of Jewish Women's Studies and Gender Issues* 13 (2007), pp. 155–82

Fischer, Michael, "Working through the Other: The Jewish, Spanish, Turkish, Iranian, Ukrainian, Lithuanian, and German unconscious of Polish culture or one hand clapping: Dialogue, silences and the mourning of Polish romanticism," in G. Marcus (ed), *Perilous States* (Chicago: University of Chicago Press, 1993)

Frankova, Anita, *i have not seen a butterfly here* (Prague: The Jewish Museum, 1993)

Friedlander, Saul, *Memory, History and the Extermination of the Jews in Europe* (Bloomington: University of Indiana Press, 1996)

Fuchs, Esther (ed), *Women and the Holocaust: Narrative and Representation* (New York: University Press of America, 1999)

Giesen, Bernhard, "The trauma of perpetrators: The Holocaust as the traumatic reference of German national identity," in J. Alexander, R. Eyerman, B. Giesen, N. Smelser, and P. Sztompka (eds), *Cultural Trauma and Collective Memory* (Berkeley: University of California Press, 2004)

Gilligan, Carol, *In a Different Voice: Psychological Theory and Women's Development* (Cambridge, MA: Harvard University Press, 1982)

Gilman, Sander, *Difference and Pathology: Stereotypes of Sexuality, Race and Madness* (Ithaca: Cornell University Press, 1985)

——, *Freud, Race and Gender* (Princeton: Princeton University Press, 1993)

Goertz, Karen, "Body, trauma, and the rituals of memory: Charlotte Delbo and Ruth Kluger," in J. Epstein and L.H. LefKowitz (eds), *Shaping Losses: Cultural Memory and the Holocaust* (Chicago: University of Illinois Press, 2001)

Green, Alan, "Religion and mysticism: The case of Judaism," in J. Neusner (ed), *Take Judaism, for Example: Studies Toward the Comparison of Religions* (Chicago: University of Chicago Press, 1983)

Gruber, Ruth, *Virtually Jewish: Reinventing Jewish Culture in Europe* (Berkeley: University of California Press, 2002)

Gubar, Susan, "Empathic identification in Anne Michael's *Fugitive Pieces*: Masculinity and poetry after Auschwitz," *Signs: A Journal of Women in Culture* 28 (2002), pp. 249–77

Herbermann, Nanda, *The Blessed Abyss: Inmate #6582 in Ravensbrück Concentration Camp for Women*, trans H. Baer (Detroit, MI: Wayne State University Press, 2000)

Halbwachs, Maurice, *On Collective Memory* (Chicago: University of Chicago Press, 1992)

Heilman, Samuel, *Defenders of the Faith: Inside Ultra-Orthdoxy* (New York: Schoken Books, 1992)

Herzog, Monika, *Drawings of Ravensbrück..."hope, which lives in us eternally"* (Gesamthersetllung: Hentrich, 1993)

Hill Collins, Patricia, *Black Feminist Thought: Knowledge, Consciousness, and Empowerment* (Boston: Unwin Hyman, 1990)

Hirsch, Marianne, *Family Frames: Photography, Narrative and Postmemory* (Cambridge, MA: Harvard University Press, 1997)

——, "Projected memory: Holocaust photographs in personal and public fantasy," in M. Bal, J. Crewe, and L. Spitzer (eds), *Acts of Memory: Cultural Recall in the Present* (Hanover, NH: University Press of New England, 1999)

——, "Surviving images: Holocaust photographs and the work of postmemory," in B. Zelizer (ed), *Visual Culture and the Holocaust* (New

Jersey: Rutgers University Press, 2000)

___, and Valerie Smith, "Feminism and cultural memory: An introduction," *Signs: Journal of Women in Culture and Society* 28 (2002), pp. 3–18

Horn, David, "This norm which is not one: Reading the female body in Lombroso's anthropology," in J. Terry and J. Urla (eds), *Deviant Bodies*, pp. 19–48

Irwin-Zarecka, Iwona, *Frames of Remembrance: The Dynamics of Collective Memory* (New Brunswick: Transaction Publishers, 1994)

Jacobs, Janet, *Hidden Heritage: The Legacy of the Crypto-Jews* (Berkeley: University of California Press, 2002)

Jacobs, Steven, "Judaism and Christianity After Auschwitz," in S. Jacobs (ed), *Contemporary Jewish Religious Responses to the Shoah* (New York: University Press of America, 1993)

Jordan, Judith, Alexandra Kaplan, Jean Baker Miller, Irene Stiver, and Janet Surry, *Women's Growth In Connection: Writings from the Stone Center* (New York: Guilford Press, 1991)

Karay, Felicja, "Women in the forced labor camps," in D. Ofer and L. Weitzman (eds), *Women in the Holocaust* (New Haven: Yale University Press, 1998)

Katz, Esther and Joan Ringelheim, *Proceedings of the Conference: Women Surviving the Holocaust*, Occasional papers from the Institute for Research in History (New York, 1983)

Koontz, Claudia, "Between memory and oblivion: Concentration camps in German memory," in J. Gillis (ed), *Commemorations: The Politics of National Identity* (Princeton, NJ: Princeton University Press, 1994)

Koshar, Rudy, *From Monuments to Traces: Artifacts of German Memory, 1870–1990* (Berkeley: University of California Press, 2000)

Krause-Schmidt, Ursula and Christine Krause (eds), *Through the Eyes of the Survivors: A Guide to Ravensbrück Memorial Museum* (Stuttgart: Lagergemeinschaft Ravensbrück, 2003)

LaCapra, Dominick, "Representing the Holocaust: Reflections on the historian's debate," in S. Friedlander (ed), *Probing the Limits of Representation: National Socialism and the "Final Solution"* (Cambridge: Harvard University Press, 1992)

Langer, Lawrence, "Gendered suffering? Women in Holocaust

testimonies," in D. Ofer and L. Weitzman (eds), *Women and the Holocaust* (New Haven: Yale University Press, 1998)

Laska, Vera (ed), *Women in the Resistance and the Holocaust* (Westport, CT: Greenwood Press, 1983)

Leninthal, Edward, *Preserving Memory: The Struggle to Create America's Holocaust Museum* (New York: Viking, 1995)

Lentin, Ronit (ed), *Gender and Catastrophe* (London: Zed Books, 1997)

____, *Israel and the Daughters of the Shoah: Reoccupying the Territories of Silence* (New York: Berghahn Books, 2000)

Lipton, Sara, "The Temple is my body: Gender, carnality and Synagoga," in E. Frojmovic (ed), *Imagining the Self: Imagining the Other* (Boston: Brill, 2002)

Longman, Timothy and Theoneste Rutagengwa, "Religion, memory, and violence in Rwanda," in O. Stier and J.S. Landres (eds), *Religion, Violence, Memory and Place Religion* (Bloomington: University of Indiana Press, 2006)

Lopez, Billie and Peter Hirsch, *A Traveler's Guide to Jewish Germany* (New York: Pelican Publishing, 1998)

Milton, Sybil, "Sensitive issues about Holocaust films," in A. Grobman and D. Landes (eds), *Genocide: Critical Issues of the Holocaust* (Los Angeles: The Simon Wiesenthal Center, 1983)

____, *In Fitting Memory: The Art and Politics of Holocaust Memorials* (Detroit: Wayne State University Press, 1991)

Misztal, Barbara, "Durkheim on collective memory," *Journal of Classical Sociology* 3 (2003), pp. 125–43

Morrison, Jack, *Ravensbrück: Everyday Life in a Women's Concentration Camp 1939–45* (Princeton, NJ: Mark Weiner, 2000)

Mushkat, Marian, *Philo-semitic and Anti-Jewish Attitudes in Post Holocaust Poland* (Lewiston, NY: Edwin Mellen Press, 1992)

Nora, Pierre, (*Lieux de mémoire*) *Realms of Memory: Rethinking the French Past* (New York: Columbia University Press, 1996), pp. xv–xxiv

Oakley, Anne, "Interviewing women: A contradiction in terms," in H. Roberts (ed), *Doing Feminist Research* (London: Routledge, 1981)

Ofer, Dalia and Lenore Weitzman (eds), *Women in the Holocaust* (New Haven: Yale University Press, 1998)

Olick, Jeffrey K. and Daniel Levy, "Collective memory and cultural

constraint: Holocaust myth and rationality in German politics,"
American Sociological Review 62 (1997), pp. 921–36

___, and Joyce Robbins, "Social memory studies: From 'collective
memory' to the historical sociology of mnemonic practices," *Annual
Review of Sociology* 24 (1998), pp. 105–40

___, "Collective memory: The two cultures," *Sociological Theory* 17:3
(1999), pp. 333–48

Pellegrini, Ann, "Whiteface Performances: Race, gender, and Jewish
bodies," in J. Boyarin and D. Boyarin (eds), *Jews and Other Differences:
The New Jewish Cultural Studies* (Minneapolis: University of Minnesota
Press, 1997)

Perl, Gisela, "A doctor in Auschwitz," in C. Rittner and J. Roth (eds),
Different Voices (New York: Paragon, 1993)

Pinto, Diana, "A new Jewish identity for post 1989 Europe," JPR Policy
Paper, no 1 (1996), pp. 1–18

Ray, Larry, "Remembrance and ambiguity—sounds and spaces of klezmer
'revivals'," online paper, School of Social Policy and Social Research,
University of Kent (Canterbury, UK, 2008), pp. 1–37

Reading, Anna, *The Social Inheritance of the Holocaust: Gender, Culture and
Memory* (New York: Palgrave Macmillan, 2002)

Reinharz, Shulamit (with Lynn Davidman), *Feminist Methods in Social
Research* (New York: Oxford University Press, 1992)

Reuter, Fritz, *Jewish Worms: Rashi House and Judengasse*, trans Ursula Fritz
(Worms: Heinrich Fischer, 1991)

Ringelheim, Joan, "Women and the Holocaust: A reconsideration of
research," in C. Rittner and J. Roth (eds), *Different Voices: Women and
the Holocaust* (New York: Paragon Press, 1993)

___, "Gender and genocide: A split memory," in R. Lentin (ed), *Gender and
Catastrophe* (London: Zed Books, 1997)

___, "The split between gender and the Holocaust," in D. Ofer and
L. Weitzman (eds), *Women and the Holocaust* (New Haven: Yale
University Press, 1998)

Rittner, Carol and John Roth (eds), *Different Voices: Women and the Holocaust*
(New York: Paragon Press, 1993)

___, "Preface," in C. Rittner and J. Roth (eds), *Different Voices: Women and
the Holocaust* (New York: Paragon Press, 1993)

Rozario, Santi, " 'Disasters' and Bengladeshi women," in R. Lentin (ed), *Gender and Catastrophe* (London: Zed Books, 1997)

Saidel, Rochelle, *The Jewish Women of Ravensbrück Concentration Camp* (Madison, WI: University of Wisconsin Press, 2004)

Sancho, Nelia, "The 'Comfort Women' system in Japan during World War II: Asian women as targets of mass rape and sexual slavery by Japan," in R. Lentin (ed), *Gender and Catastrophe* (London: Zed Books, 1997)

Schreckenberg, Heinz, *The Jews in Christian Art: An Illustrated History* (New York, Continuum, 1996)

Schwartz, Barry, "The social context of commemoration: A study in collective memory," *Social Forces* 62 (1982), pp. 374–402

——, "Social change and collective memory: The democratization of George Washington," *American Sociological Review* 56 (1991), pp. 221–36

——, "Memory as a cultural system: Abraham Lincoln in World War II," *American Sociological Review* 61 (1996), pp. 908–27

Sered, Susan, *What Makes Women Sick? Maternity, Modesty and Militarism in Israeli Society* (Hanover, NH: Brandeis University Press, 2000)

Sex-Zwangsarbeit in NS-Konzentrationslagern: Katalog zur Ausstellung (Vienna: Die Aussteller-Verein zur Foerderung von Historischen und Kunsthistorischen Ausstellungen, 2006)

Smolen, Kazimierz, *Guide Book: State Museum in Oświęcim* (Oświęcim, Poland, 1999)

Sontag, Susan, *Regarding the Pain of Others* (New York: Farrar, Straus, Giroux, 2003)

Stacey, Judith, "Can there be a feminist ethnography?" *Women's Studies International Forum* 11 (1988), pp. 21–7

Stelling, Alison, Andrew Charlesworth, Robert Guzik and Michal Paszkowski, "A tale of two institutions: Shaping Oświęcim-Auschwitz," *Geoforum* 39 (2008), pp. 401–3

Stern, Frank, "German-Jewish relations in the postwar period: The ambiguities of anti-Semitic and philosemitic discourse," in Y.M. Bodemann (ed), *Jews, Germans, Memory: Reconstructions of Jewish Life in Germany* (Ann Harbor: University of Michigan Press, 1996)

Stier, Oren and J. Shawn Landres (eds), *Religion, Violence, Memory and Place Religion* (Bloomington: University of Indiana Press, 2006)

Stiglmayer, Alexandra (ed), *The War Against Women in Bosnia-Herzegovina* (Lincoln, NE: University of Nebraska Press, 1994)

Struk, Janina, *Photographing the Holocaust* (London: I.B.Tauris, 2004)

Strzelecka, Irena, "Women," in Y. Gutman and M. Berenbaum (eds), *Anatomy of the Auschwitz Death Camp* (Bloomington: Indiana University Press, 1998)

Sztompka, Piotr, "The trauma of social change: A case of post Communist societies," in J. Alexander, R. Eyerman, B. Giesen, N. Smelser, and P. Sztompka (eds), *Cultural Trauma and Collective Memory* (Berkeley: University of California Press, 2004)

Terry, Jennifer and Jacqueline Urla (eds), *Deviant Bodies* (Bloomington: Indiana University Press, 1995)

Trachtenberg, Joshua, *The Devil and the Jews: The Medieval Conception of the Jew and Its Relation to Modern Anti-Semitism* (New Haven: Yale University Press, 1943)

Trevor-Roper, Hugh, *The European Witch-Craze of the Sixteenth and Seventeenth Centuries and Other Essays* (New York: Harper Collins, 1967)

Tyndall, Andrea, "Memory, authenticity and replication of the Shoah in museums," in R. Lentin (ed), *Representing the Shoah for the Twenty-first Century* (New York: Berghahn Books, 2004)

Unger, Michal, "The status and plight of women in the Lodz ghetto," in D. Ofer and L. Weitzman (eds), *Women in the Holocaust* (New Haven: Yale University Press, 1998)

Wasserfall, Rahel (ed), *Women and Water: Menstruation in Jewish Life and Law* (Hanover, NH: Brandeis University Press, 1999)

Wiedmer, Caroline, *The Claims of Memory: Representations of the Holocaust in Contemporary Germany and France* (Ithaca: Cornell University Press, 1999)

Wistrich, Robert, *Demonizing the Other: Anti-Semitism, Racism and Xenophobia* (The Netherlands: Harwood Academic Publishers, 1999)

Wolf, Diane, *Beyond Anne Frank: Hidden Children and Postwar Families in Holland* (Berkeley: University of California Press, 2007)

Young, James, *The Texture of Memory: Holocaust Memorials and Meanings* (New Haven: Yale University Press, 1993)

Zelizer, B. (ed), *Visual Culture and the Holocaust* (New Jersey: Rutgers University Press, 2001)

____, "Women in Holocaust photography," in B. Zelizer (ed), *Visual Culture and the Holocaust* (New Jersey: Rutgers University Press, 2001)

Zubrzycki, Genevieve, *The Crosses of Auschwitz: Nationalism and Religion in Post Communist Poland* (Chicago: University of Chicago Press, 2006)

INDEX

Numbers in **bold** refer to illustrations.